MORE POWER TO YOU!

The Personal Protection Handbook for Women

MORE POWER TO YOU!

The Personal Protection Handbook for Women

Samantha Koumanelis

Round Lake Publishing

Ridgefield, Connecticut

Round Lake Publishing Co.
31 Bailey Avenue
Ridgefield, CT 06877

Printed in the United States of America

0987654321

ISBN 0-929543-21-1

Important Note to the Readers of this Book

The information in this book is intended to provide readers with suggestions for protecting themselves and their families. No advice, however, can guarantee safety and because each case is different, any advice must be tempered with the common sense of the individual in a given situation. Readers are also cautioned to familiarize themselves with the applicable federal laws and the laws in their own states and municipalities regarding the use of self-protection methods, particularly physical self-defense, the use of weapons—including fire arms, and self-defense sprays such as tear gas and mace.

This book does not advocate the use of weapons or physical self-defense as a means of self-protection. Instead, it recommends the avoidance of circumstances which might put individuals in potentially harmful situations.

Introduction

My upbringing was not much different from that of most women I have talked with. My parents' objective was to make sure my sisters and I grew up to be "young ladies." We were taught to be loving, nurturing, kind and gentle.

Our self-defense training as children was limited to one warning—don't talk to strangers.

However, my parents did make it a point to teach my brothers how to identify and protect themselves from potentially dangerous situations. Daughters, they believed, had no need for such information because there would always be a man nearby to protect them.

So, we girls grew up hoping we'd never have to deal with crime, and if an occasion did arise when we needed to, we'd look around for a strong male to help us out. The contradiction, we discovered, was that often there was no man around to protect us. Or worse yet, at times the man who *was* around was not there to protect us—he was there to do us harm.

Who to turn to but ourselves? For in the final analysis, we soon discovered, we would have to take responsibility for our own safety and well-being.

My two sisters, Beverly and Janet, did grow up to be fine young ladies. I became a private investigator with a Black Belt in karate.

As an undercover investigator, I experienced first-hand the countless ways criminals size up potential victims. I learned how they administer tests to prospective targets to see if they meet certain criteria—then decide whether to select them as their victims.

In the battle against crime, knowledge is a powerful weapon. There's a lot to be learned about how we leave ourselves open to being victimized. I've written this book to share my knowledge with you.

In it I describe what I've discovered through years of experience, both on the job and off, and I explain how to recognize, avoid, and deal with dangerous situations.

Through my personal protection seminars and workshops, I've spoken to thousands of women across the country who represent all age groups and every walk of life. These women have shared their stories, fears and concerns with me. *More Power to You!* addresses those fears and concerns and lays out the simple steps you can take to be responsible for your own self-protection, while feeling safer and more confident in the process.

I encourage you to do all that you can to keep from being victimized— whether you're at home, at work, or anywhere else—while maintaining your uniqueness and leading a full life.

Acknowledgments

No book worth reading has ever been completed without the hard work of talented and patient people. This book is no exception. It started out as nothing more than some notes scribbled down hastily on anything I could find, whenever I felt a moment of inspiration.

The good people at Round Lake Publishing encouraged me to organize my notes into a manuscript. They believed in me and in the subject matter enough to send me a book contract.

Thanks to my editor Carole Lefcort who, with her sharp eye for detail and an unswerving sense of humor, turned my disorganized thoughts into a clear, concise and easy to read book that any author would be proud to claim as her own.

Thanks to my family and friends, whose continuous support (i.e., nagging—and you know who you are) made me work harder and faster to complete this project.

And, thanks to all of you who have attended my workshops. You requested and encouraged me to take the time to share more of my information in a book. I did it for you.

Contents

More Power . . . on the Street

More Power . . . at Home

More Power . . . at Work

More Power . . . When Traveling

More Power . . .
On the Street

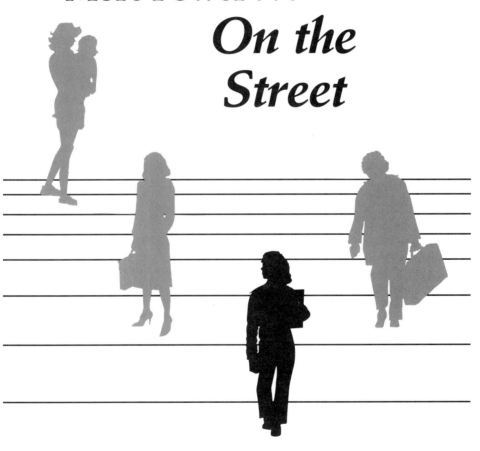

Chapter 1

❖❖❖❖❖

Street Smarts

In the U.S., a violent crime is committed every 19 seconds. Someone is murdered every 24 minutes, raped every six minutes, robbed every 55 seconds, assaulted every 33 seconds. In the time it's taking you to read this paragraph, at least one violent crime was committed.

There is a formula for crime. D + O = C (Desire + Opportunity = Crime). In order for a crime to be committed, someone must want to commit a crime and must also have the opportunity to commit it. Without both of these components, no crime will be committed.

Most of us believe that street crime is completely random in nature. We believe that we become victims *only* when we happen to be in the wrong place at the wrong time. But the fact is that crime is *not* completely random and we *do* have a degree of control over whether or not we are chosen as victims.

HOW NOT TO BE A VICTIM

Too many women operate under the false assumption that crime (mugging, sexual assault, robbery) is something that can only happen to others. It's not something that can happen to them because they're too short, too tall, too fat, too old, too young or too something else.

In fact, the likelihood that you will be victimized has less to do with the way you look than the way you are perceived from the criminal's point of view. Often a woman becomes a victim because of one or more of these factors:

- She isn't paying attention to what's going on around her.

- Her body language indicates to the criminal that she would make a good victim.
- She happens to be in the wrong place at the wrong time.

TESTING YOUR VICTIM POTENTIAL

How likely are you to become a victim? Take this test to see if you are potentially vulnerable:

1. Do you walk with your eyes focused on the pavement?
2. Do you carry your pocketbook dangling from your wrist, or slung carelessly over your shoulder?
3. Do you walk around with headphones glued to your ears?
4. Do you stop to give directions or the time of day to anyone who asks?
5. When you feel vulnerable, do you walk with mincing steps and try to make yourself look as small as possible?
6. If you spot trouble, do you react, or do you continue on as usual and just hope for the best?

Well, how did you do? For a perfect score, "No" should be the answer to all six questions. Even one "Yes" could get you into trouble. We'll go over your responses to each question and give you some tips on how you can remove the opportunities for crime. Read the suggestions carefully to learn how to recognize and avoid potentially dangerous situations. Remember: If there is no opportunity, there is no crime!

Keep your head up. If you focus on the pavement, you can't be aware of your surroundings. Muggers set their radar on those who send out signals of vulnerability. If you walk down the street looking preoccupied, you are especially vulnerable to crime.

Make eye contact with people. You don't need to do it with everyone who passes you, and you shouldn't stare down a person, since that's confrontational. But by no means should you turn your eyes away from someone who is looking directly at you. Averting your eyes from someone tells them that you are vulnerable—that they make you feel uneasy, or that you are afraid of them.

You are most susceptible to attack if you limit your vision to within a few feet of yourself. Any action against you requires instant response, which you will be unable to make if you're not paying attention to your environment.

Mind your handbag. There is nothing more tempting to a thief than a woman who is careless about how she carries her handbag, whether it's dangling loosely from her wrist or thoughtlessly tossed over her shoulder. What's a thief to do when the prospect of an easy score is within reach? Grab it, of course.

If you don't want to lose your handbag, you must be aware of it at all times. Never allow yourself to be distracted by the antics criminals perform to draw your attention away from your bag. (See page 9 for more information about the do's and don'ts of carrying your purse.)

Skip that tune. Walking with headphones on your ears, tuned into music or a self-help tape, may be relaxing, but it provides the criminal with a great way to catch a victim. If you are not paying attention to what's going on around you, a criminal could sneak up behind you and catch you by surprise. If you had been paying attention, you might have denied him that opportunity.

Stay in motion. Giving directions or the time to strangers is not necessarily a bad practice, if you don't have to stand still to do it. Once you allow a stranger to stop you in your tracks, you leave yourself open to possible danger such as a mugging, purse snatching or sexual assault.

If a criminal is unsure of whether you will make a good victim, one who can be taken by surprise and will offer no resistance, there are several methods he can use to stop you and size you up.

What should you do if someone stops directly in front of you and wants to know the time? Either give the approximate time or say you don't know the time, while walking around the person as you speak.

You could be in trouble if you use both your hands to tell the time—one to draw your watch toward you and the other to push up your sleeve. You'd have to release your grip on your purse, making it accessible to the purse snatcher.

If someone calls you over and asks for directions from a car, stay on the sidewalk and respond from there. *Don't* go over to the car, because once you lean your head into his window to hear what he's saying, he's got you! *Never* approach a stranger's car!

Whatever the method, the aim is the same—to get you to stop and talk. Once you have stopped to respond to a criminal's request, whether he asks for the time, directions or for some change, he's got you. Often the questions are accompanied by deliberate bumbling to see how gullible you may be. The next step may be to ask you a personal question such as your name, where you live, or where you're going. If you are uncomfortable, he will sense it and know that you will be a good victim.

Walk like a winner. Don't transmit vulnerability through your walk. The "wimp walk" transmits to criminals that you are afraid and unsure. Stand tall, keep your head held high, use long, brisk strides and telegraph a comfortable, expansive attitude. Let your body language do the talking and make it say that you are self-assured, alert and not a good target. Be natural, but confident.

Trust your instincts. Don't willfully walk into a threatening situation when the little voice inside your head warns you to run the other way. If you are walking down the street and sense that there may be trouble ahead, don't pretend that everything is fine. If your internal warning system goes off, pay attention to it. Ignoring the warning may put you in jeopardy.

If you must pass by a gang, make eye contact with them without losing your confident stride and without hugging your handbag closer to your body. If you spot them in time, cross the street or slip into a crowded shop, if possible, without being obvious. The best advice is to stay out of gang-infested areas. However, if they are a part of your neighborhood, get to know the enemy. Make yourself aware of the gang members and avoid them.

If someone is following you on foot and you cannot elude him, scream "Fire." That should bring people to the scene and scare away the offender. While on foot, if you are being followed by someone in a car, turn around and walk in the opposite direction. Try to find a store or gas station where you can go for help.

BEATING THE PLAYERS AT THEIR OWN GAMES

Street criminals fall into one of several general categories. Here's an introduction to the types of criminals you're most likely to meet and a description of how they usually operate.

Muggers. To get what they want from you, these criminals resort to the use of force or the threat of violence. The crime they commit is called "personal robbery." It differs from purse-snatching and pickpocketing, which are called "personal larceny," in which no force or violence is used.

Muggers often work alone. They choose the best time and place to commit their crimes, and plan their escape route long before an intended victim comes on the scene. On some occasions, they work with an accomplice who engages the victim in a conversation (asking for directions or the time, for example) while the mugger comes up from behind and grabs a purse, jewelry or any other valuables.

Because a mugger relies on force to get what he wants, he almost always carries a weapon. You shouldn't try to resist these criminals or you could be seriously injured or even killed. Just because you don't see a weapon, doesn't mean there isn't one.

If an armed attacker wants your possessions, give them up. If he intends to do you bodily harm, use your head and try to talk your way out of the situation. Do anything that might throw the attacker off balance. Be prepared with a line like, "Oh, I'm so glad to see you!" Or , "Didn't you go to school with my son?" Or even try acting crazy—talk out loud to an imaginary presence or look up into the sky and babble!

If the weapon is a gun, *never* try to fight back. Try to remain cool and calm and avoid any sudden movements or sounds that could provoke your assailant to pull the trigger.

Favorite mugging locations are dark doorways, hallways, elevators, parks and automated teller machine sites.

Purse-snatchers. The only requirement these criminals have is a "good victim," meaning someone who won't give chase or offer resistance. The purse-snatcher can be anyone—from an eight year old child to a senior citizen—and he is likely to work alone. Once he grabs your handbag, briefcase or package, he runs quickly into concealment.

Unlike the mugger who carefully plans the time and location of his crime, the purse-snatcher is less systematic, working day and night, indoors and out. Once money or other valuables are removed from a snatched purse, the purse is usually discarded.

Pickpockets. Endowed with skilled hands and using nothing more than a handkerchief and newspaper as tools of the trade, these thieves are probably the most sophisticated of all. They operate best in crowded areas such as shopping malls, fairs and carnivals, movie theaters, airline and bus terminals and on public transportation. The crowded bus or train allows the pickpocket to get close to his victim without raising a lot of suspicion.

Often a pickpocket, working with one or more accomplices, will spot his intended victim and signal to a partner who then distracts the victim by bumping into her and apologizing profusely for his clumsiness. At the same time, he is snatching her wallet, perhaps passing it to a third accomplice to keep suspicion away from himself.

Pickpockets are creative thieves. They have been known to help further their own purposes by making announcements over loud speakers warning the public of pickpockets in the crowd, and reminding people to check that their handbags and wallets are secure.

Spotters watch as men pat their jackets or pants pockets, checking to be sure their wallets are still in place, and see which women hug their purses. This tells them where the men's wallets are kept and which women are carrying something of value in their purses.

STREET SAVVY GUIDELINES

The following general safety measures will also help you avoid muggings, purse-snatchings and sexual assaults.

- Avoid walking through deserted streets, alleys and unpopulated parks. Try to avoid unfamiliar areas.
- Walk nearer to the curb, away from bushes, doorways and fences, which provide cover for someone who is stalking a victim.
- Always remain within lighted areas at night.
- Never accept rides from strangers. (Sounds obvious, but people still do it!)
- If you must go out alone at night, tell someone where you're going and when you expect to return.
- Wait for buses, taxis and trains in well-lighted, well-populated areas. If given a choice, don't board a bus or train if there are no other passengers. If you must board a bus or train without passengers, sit up front near the driver or conductor, but not in an inside seat next to the window. You do not want someone to come in and trap you in your seat.
  If you must wait for the train in a deserted station, stand well back from the edge of the platform.
- If you jog, walk, or bike, vary your routes and times, avoiding isolated trails. If possible, go with a partner. Again, let someone know your route and when to expect your return.
- Leave the jewelry and headphones home. If you jog before dawn or after dark, wear reflective clothing.
- Use your intuition. If you feel uneasy about a person or place, avoid it.

- Carry identification inside your shoe, as well as change for a phone call.

CHOOSING THE SAFEST HANDBAG

Now let's talk a little more about your handbag—your third arm, your lifeline. One of the best ways to remove the opportunity for having your handbag stolen is to stop carrying one! Easier said than done? What would you do with all its contents? Think about it. Do you really need everything that's in your handbag every time you leave your house?

Do you carry a purse out of need or just out of habit? And what do you keep in your absolutely necessary, can't live without it, purse? Probably a handy all-purpose wallet that holds all your credit cards, cash, checkbook and more, all in one place.

The bad news is that pickpockets love these all-purpose wallets. With one simple grab, they can take everything. It saves them from having to sort through all your things to get to the good stuff. If you feel you have to carry checks, credit cards and cash, at least diversify. Keep them in separate places. Don't make it easy for the pickpocket.

Be sure to record the numbers of all the credit cards, licenses, and other important documents you carry. Keep this list in a safe place at home or in a safe deposit box.

If you must carry a purse, consider wearing a fanny pack or waist pouch. They are small, are worn around your waist and allow you to have two free hands.

You never have to worry about leaving a fanny pack behind because it remains securely fastened around your waist. A word of caution: Secure the belt under your coat, not over it, and under your shirt or sweater if you can. This affords an extra measure of protection for you and an added annoyance factor for a thief.

Because it is not as spacious as a regular handbag, the fanny pack will force you to pare down and carefully select only the most essential items. Once you get used to having two free hands and no added weight on your shoulders, you won't want to switch back to a regular handbag again.

It's true that waist pouches may not be the most attractive accessories to wear over a suit or fancy dress, that they are more appropriate for casual wear. If style is that important to you, or wearing anything around your waist makes you uncomfortable, and you absolutely must have a handbag, then learn the do's and don'ts of carrying one, which follows.

Choose something sturdy. The best handbag to carry (next to the fanny pack) is a leather or canvas one with thick, sturdy straps, not too large and cumbersome, and with zippered pockets and compartments. In order to carry this purse securely, rest the bag comfortably at the waist or no lower than your hip, with the zipper or clasp in front, and keep your hand securely clasped over the closure.

Don't wrap the strap around your wrist a few hundred times thinking that will protect you from purse snatchers. It won't. If they want your bag badly enough they'll take it—along with your wrist, your arm, your shoulder, and whatever else it's attached to.

Keep your purse close to your body, whether the strap is across your chest or over your shoulder.

Avoid clutches. The worst handbag to carry is a clutch purse. It can only be carried in one of two ways: under your arm (where the purse-snatcher has no trouble grabbing it), or clasped in one hand. This ties up one hand and no matter how tightly you think you're holding on to it, it will never be tight enough to stop a thief.

If you must carry a clutch purse, carry it upside down with your hand on the clasp. That way, if you feel a tug you can unfasten the clasp and watch everything roll down the sidewalk. Time will work against the thief. He probably won't want to chase after all your things to pick up your wallet.

Make it hard to open. Another poor choice of handbag is one with just a flap over the front, or one with just a snap (which you might or might not remember to close) and no inside zipper compartments.

If you carry one of these bags, consider giving it up for a more secure bag. But if you insist on carrying this type of purse, don't sling it over your shoulder—especially with the flap side facing out. You might as well stand on a street corner, open up your bag and invite everyone to stop, reach in and take whatever they want. Instead, keep the flap side next to you and hold your bag close to your body.

Don't try to outsmart a thief. Hiding your purse inside another bag— a straw or canvas tote, perhaps—won't fool a professional. A thief knows your purse is in there. And he appreciates how much easier you've made his job because of the way you carry it.

Since the handles aren't long enough to reach around your shoulders, you hold on to the handles and swing your bag to and fro as you walk. It provides the perfect opportunity for any thief, beginner or pro, to come up behind you and yank your bag away on the back swing.

KEEPING YOUR HANDBAG TO YOURSELF

Whatever type of purse you choose to carry, hold on to it. Never leave your purse on the floor at your feet or hanging from coat hooks, on the backs of chairs or on bar stools. Always have it in clear view, either on top of the table or in your lap.

If you are in a restaurant and plan to check out the salad bar or buffet table, take your purse with you. Don't think you can fool a thief by putting your bag under your coat on the chair next to you, or on the floor mixed in with your other packages.

When you visit the ladies room, where do you put your handbag? If you're like most women, you hang it from the hook on the back of the door. All a thief has to do is reach over the door and take it. With your pantyhose down around your knees, you're in no position to give chase.

Instead of hanging your bag from the door, place it on the toilet tank or keep it on the shelf provided. If neither of these options is available, keep it over your shoulder. Although it may be awkward to maneuver this way, at least your bag is safe.

If you are at the beauty salon, at the movies, at a sporting event or concert, on a bus, train, or plane, keep your handbag with you, in your lap—not on the floor, unattended, where someone can hook the strap and drag it away.

Avoid overloading yourself with a briefcase and handbag or with packages. If you carry a briefcase, put a small purse and cosmetic bag inside it. And if you have your arms full, *don't* let your handbag dangle from your wrist or elbow. Try to consolidate your packages so that you have one arm free.

Carry your briefcase or purse on the side of your body facing traffic rather than pedestrians. (If you travel abroad, the opposite is true; carry your bag on the building side, away from traffic and the prevalent motor scooter purse-snatchers.)

Never leave your purse or packages unattended in a shopping cart, or on the roof of your car while you buckle up your kids in the back seat. And in the car, your handbag should go on the floor, not on the seat next to you where its visibility makes it a temptation.

Walk confidently and stay alert. Purse-snatchers like to catch you off-guard or preoccupied. If they know you are aware of them, they'll look around for someone else who they can take by surprise.

When a Purse-Snatcher Strikes

What should you do if you are grabbed and forced to hand over your purse? There's no simple answer to this question because the possibilities are so numerous. You are the only one who can evaluate a particular situation.

As a rule, give in to all of the criminal's demands. Give up the handbag willingly and quickly. There is *nothing* in your purse that's worth risking your life for. See Chapter 5 for a discussion of self-defense alternatives.

Resisting street robbery is simply not wise. There are women in hospitals across the country recovering from beatings and broken bones they suffered because they refused to give up their purses. And those are the lucky ones— they didn't lose their lives.

One way you may get to keep your wallet is to carry "mugger money"— cash that you can take out of your pocket and hand over quickly.

Don't tell your assailant you have no money if, in fact, you do, and don't assume you're safe if you carry no cash. "Mugger money" could save your life if you come up against a psychotic criminal who would shoot you for having empty pockets.

If a thief is successful in getting your purse, don't play the heroine by taking revenge into your own hands. Call the police and let them do their job. Give a detailed description of your assailant: age, height, weight, coloring, what he was wearing and any distinguishing marks such as tattoos, scars, mustache or beard. Be sure to tell the police the direction in which he fled. Also do the following:

- Let the police know if your purse contained keys and any identification. Criminals can use them to commit robbery.
- If your keys were taken, change your locks as soon as possible, including the locks on your car.
- Advise your bank if your checkbook or passbook was stolen. Notify the credit card companies of the theft immediately.
- If your Social Security card was stolen, notify the Social Security Administration of the theft immediately and obtain a new number. With your Social Security number, a criminal can apply to obtain your Social Security benefits, welfare benefits, credit cards in your name or even your paycheck. An impersonator can destroy

your credit rating and create criminal records in your name. See more about this in the section on shopping beginning on page 15.

- If an address book was in your handbag, it's a good idea to tell those friends whose names were listed that you were robbed. Criminals use these names to set people up for various scams, swindles and burglaries.

Chapter 2

❖❖❖❖❖

Safe Shopping

Where can one find a great number of women in a concentrated area, all of whom are carrying money? Why, at the shopping mall, of course! Unfortunately, malls are a favorite haunt for thieves and other criminals.

And if you pay for a purchase by check or credit card, you may inadvertently be giving away more personal information than you realize—or than is even necessary. Information that, in the wrong hands, could turn a tidy profit for someone, at your expense.

We'll look at both these shopping challenges in this chapter.

MALL MENACES

Malls may *appear* to be safe because there are so many people around, but in fact they are a haven for thieves. The targets are plentiful and there are many escape routes for criminals.

Tempting merchandise, soothing music and climate-controlled, plant-filled walkways encourage shoppers to let down their guard. The preoccupied crowds provide choice victims for shoplifters, muggers and even rapists.

How can you protect yourself at the mall? The most important rule is to stay alert and pay attention to what's going on around you.

Here are some danger spots and tips on protecting yourself:

Parking lots. The majority of crimes at shopping malls actually take place in the parking lot. The vast, car-filled lots offer camouflage to criminals looking for cars to steal or victims to prey upon.

Mall lots that are close to highways are tailor-made for smooth escapes.

But actually, most of the crime involves the theft of valuables from cars. Follow these simple rules when in a mall parking lot:

- If you have packages or other valuables in your car, lock them in the trunk. Packages visible in a car are more likely to be stolen.
- Whenever possible, avoid parking in underground garages. And park as close as possible to the mall entrance.
- Always lock your car, whether you have packages in it or not.
- When you return to your car, have your key in your hand, check both front and back seats before entering your car, and lock the doors immediately after you get in.
- Don't put your shopping bags on the car roof while you search your purse for your keys, and don't leave your purse on the seat next to an unlocked door while you go around to the trunk with your bags.

Stairwells. Muggers and rapists sometimes lurk in little-used stairwells. Stay away from areas that are not well-traveled or well lighted.

Elevators. They are the perfect place to become a victim. All a criminal needs to do is press the "Stop" button and he's got you all to himself.

Think twice before getting into an elevator with only one stranger or with a disreputable looking group. Wait for the next elevator.

Restrooms. Try not to use isolated, empty restrooms, for obvious reasons. However, if you have no choice, remember to keep your purse and packages close to you, either on the toilet tank behind you or over your shoulder or arm, not hanging on the hook on the door.

Dressing rooms with curtains. Don't leave your purse on the floor. Hang it on the hook in the dressing room and put your clothes on top of it. This will keep a thief from reaching under the curtain and snatching it. If you leave the cubicle, even for just a moment, take your purse with you.

Clothes racks. When you are making selections from a rack of clothing, have a friend hold your purse for you or hang on to it yourself. (Here's where a fanny pack comes in especially handy—two free hands, no inconvenience, no worry.)

Cash registers. Often, this is where a criminal selects his victim. Flash a large wad of bills and you may be followed out of the store and robbed. Carry only what you need and don't flash your money.

Crowded areas. Women being bumped and shoved in a crowd often fail to notice when a hand slips into their purse. Stay alert. (See chapter 1 for the best and worst handbags to carry.)

Restaurants. The fast food line is a pickpocket's paradise. Your mind is on what to order, his is on making a quick score. When seated, keep your purse off the back of the chair and in your lap.

Automated cash machines. These have become choice locations for thieves and muggers. Don't use the machine if someone is loitering nearby. He may be trying to see your code number or waiting to relieve you of the cash you are withdrawing.

A con artist may try to pass himself off as a bank official. Dressed for the part, he may explain that there have been complaints about the machine not working properly. He will then ask to use your card to see if he can get it to work, and request your private code number. Don't fall for this scam! Take your card and report the incident to bank security or the police.

PAYING PITFALLS

How many times, when you have written a personal check for a purchase, has the store clerk asked for two forms of identification—and then written your credit card number on your check? How many times have you been asked to put your address and telephone number on a credit card sales slip?

Merchants across the country are violating consumer privacy and exposing their customers to potential credit fraud with their check acceptance and credit card policies.

Quite often when you write a check to pay for a purchase, the sales clerk will ask for one or more of your major credit cards and your driver's license, and will copy the numbers onto the back of your check. This leaves you open to mail order fraud, in which someone uses your credit card number to order merchandise by phone or through the mail. Or it can lead to application fraud, in which someone steals your personal information and applies for credit in your name and then runs up large bills.

When you allow a salesperson to write your credit card and driver's license numbers on the back of your check for identification, you have put your bank account number, signature, name, address, telephone number, plus credit card numbers all on one piece of paper that will pass through many hands. This can be very useful to anyone who intends to use your personal data for illicit purposes. The idea is to keep these types of identifying data as segregated as possible to prevent anyone from impersonating you.

SOCIAL SECURITY SCAMS

In several states, an individual's Social Security number is used as the identifying number on a driver's license. A criminal can take your Social Security number and, for a tidy profit, sell it on the black market to illegal aliens. To be employed in this country, you must give an employer your Social Security number to prove you are a citizen of the U.S.

Using your Social Security number, a criminal can get credit cards, car loans, employment, etc. Your Social Security number can reveal a wealth of information to criminals who know how to break into the Government's computer system. It identifies the banks and account numbers of your checking and savings accounts; it reveals any and all investments, real estate holdings, welfare, medical and government benefits, pensions, and number of dependents; it enables someone to receive your retirement money, cash in your IRA's and tax refund, and can cause general mayhem by allowing someone to intercept your mail or assume your identity. Privacy experts say the incidence of Social Security fraud is so vast there is no way to measure it.

What should you do if someone asks for your Social Security number? First, remember this number is your private information and don't give it out to everyone who asks for it. Decide who is entitled to have this information— bank officers, prospective employers, insurance companies, legitimate stock brokers and so forth. Keep your number from those who have no right to know it—sales clerks, survey takers, kennels, libraries, auto repair shops, etc.

Stand firm when you refuse to give out your number and don't allow anyone to coerce you into revealing it. The result may be that you are refused a sale or service. Explain your rights to someone in charge. If you are still refused, ask for the name and address of the president or owner of the company. Send a letter stating that you will no longer be doing business with a company that violates your privacy.

CREDIT CARD TABOOS

What about your rights where credit card numbers are concerned? You may refuse to allow a merchant to write your credit card number on your personal check, but as with your Social Security number, there is nothing that prevents the merchant from refusing the sale.

According to BankCard Holders of America, an agency specifically designed to deal with consumer fraud and privacy protection, you may offer to show the merchant that you do indeed hold a major credit card. Have it noted on the check which card it is: Visa, MasterCard, American Express, and so forth, without having its number taken down.

What should you do if you are refused a sale because of your unwillingness to have your credit card number recorded on your check? Tell the clerk you would like to speak with the store or department manager. Explain to the manager that you are concerned about the risks of credit card fraud, and point out that:

- Visa, MasterCard and American Express operating rules strictly prohibit merchants from charging a credit card to cover a bounced check.
- Merchants have all the information they need to locate the consumer if there is a problem with the check— name, address, phone number and driver's license. In most cases they may not use the credit card number to locate the customer.

Merchants frequently ask consumers to write their phone numbers and addresses on credit card sales slips when processing bank credit card transactions. This may also compromise your privacy. For example, if you are paying extra money every month on your phone bill for an unpublished number, why should you give it out to someone you don't know?

Did you know that merchants can *sell* your name and telephone number to telemarketers? If you want to cut down on those annoying phone calls, *stop giving out your phone number!* (And don't have it printed on your checks.)

Requiring your phone number on the credit slip as a condition of sale is actually *prohibited* by American Express, MasterCard and Visa. Merchants do *not* need your phone number because they are relieved of financial liability by the cardholder's bank. If there is a problem with the transaction, the card issuing bank absorbs the loss. If a clerk insists on having your phone number and/or address on the card slip, and you don't have the time to explain the facts, give them your work address and phone number, or make up an address and phone number, *but don't use your own!*

Realize you *do* have choices. The charge card companies prohibit merchants from refusing your sale just because you refuse to provide personal information on your charge slip.

For more information about protecting your rights, send $3.00 to:

BankCard Holders of America
560 Herndon Parkway - Suite 120
Herndon, VA 22070
(703) 481-1110

Ask for the "Privacy and Fraud Protection" pamphlet and a wallet-sized card on your rights as a consumer.

Chapter 3

❖❖❖❖❖

Safety on Wheels

The car you have come to depend on for business or pleasure can leave you stranded and in dangerous situations. It can also cause you a tremendous amount of grief or injury unless you take certain steps to protect your vehicle and yourself when you're traveling in it.

For these reasons it's imperative that you make time to give your car regular preventive checkups and that you learn how to keep your car (and its contents) from being victimized.

You also need to protect yourself from being victimized if you decide to sell your car privately or if you are buying a used car. We'll discuss both subjects in this chapter.

MAINTAINING A DEPENDABLE CAR

Maintain your vehicle according to the manufacturer's manual, which you should keep in the glove compartment and refer to *before* problems arise.

Learn what properly inflated tires look like and check periodically for nails, tread wear and slow leaks. Keep an inflated spare tire, jack, jumper cables, a scraper for ice, a brush for snow removal and traction aids for ice or mud all in your trunk. You don't want to be stranded in a car that can't be driven. Also have a flashlight and first aid kit as well as a spare fan belt and replacement fuses in the car at all times.

Be attuned to how your car sounds and handles. Any variation from what you're used to could signal possible problems. You should have your car checked out by a mechanic as soon as you notice something unusual. It's also a good idea to subscribe to one of the emergency road services, such as AAA, which can jump start your car if your battery dies or tow you to a service station if necessary.

Each time you get into your car, check the gas gauge. One of the most common causes of car problems is running out of gas. Know how far you can go on a quarter, a half and a full tank of gas. Never let your gas tank get close to being empty. Think of your tank as being empty when it reads half-full.

SAFEGUARDING YOUR CAR

According to the FBI Crime Index, in 1990 1,635,900 cars were stolen—amounting to a loss of 8 billion dollars. It's big business in this country.

Many cars are stolen because they're easy to break into and lack anti-theft protection. Consider installing one or more anti-theft devices to make it difficult, if not impossible, to steal your car. Here are some anti-theft devices that will foil the amateur thief and hamper the pro:

Kill switch. It's like having a second ignition switch. Your car won't start unless a hidden switch is activated.

Fuel switch. It closes a valve to cut off the fuel supply.

Armored collar. A metal shield that locks around the steering column and covers the ignition.

Steering wheel lock. One brand, called "The Club," features a long steel bar which locks onto the steering wheel, preventing it from turning. Another kind of device has a bar which locks the steering wheel to the brake pedal. A lock of this type, made by the Kryptonite Corporation, comes with a guarantee that if your car is stolen while their lock is in place, the company will pay you $1,000 toward your insurance deductible.

Alarm system. Sounds a loud noise if your car is tampered with or jostled. It sometimes comes as standard equipment with a new car or may be installed by alarm specialists.

Stolen vehicle recovery system. A tracking device is activated when the vehicle is stolen. This tells the tracking station the vehicle's identification and location, and the direction in which it is traveling to help the police locate it.

Vehicle identification methods. Use one of the following methods to help police and insurance companies identify your car if thieves obscure the manufacturer's original identification numbers:

- Etch the VIN (Vehicle Identification Number) in several hard-to-find spots, using an electric etcher.

- Write your name, address and VIN, using a permanent marker, under the hood or trunk.
- Hide business cards or home address labels under the floor mats or seats or drop them down window channels into the door interior.

You can pay anywhere from a few dollars to several hundred dollars for anti-theft devices. In choosing a system, take into account your personal budget, the make and model of your car and the auto theft rate in your area. Once you've bought a safety device, let an expert install it. Amateur installations are relatively easy to defeat.

When you buy a new car, check the manufacturer's list of options for anti-theft devices. Be aware, however, that with a "standard" security system (one that is installed on each car of a model line), car thieves may learn how to defeat the system, sometimes after practicing on just one car.

Remember: Any anti-theft device is only as good as the person who remembers to use it.

DISCOURAGING CAR THIEVES

Eighty percent of all the cars that are stolen are unlocked at the time; forty percent of them actually have the keys still in the ignition.

If you lock up and pocket the keys (even if you'll only be gone a few minutes), most thieves won't bother breaking in—unless, of course, you have something of value in plain view to tempt them.

A car doesn't have to be new and shiny to attract a car thief. Most thieves don't care what kind of car they take, as long as it's easy to steal. Even though your car may seem ordinary, the professional thief may have his eye on it simply because his car-theft ring has an order for one like it or a ready market for the parts.

> Kathy, excited over her brand new Pontiac Firebird, stopped outside her friend Rick's apartment to show off the new car. She dashed up the front steps and rang Rick's bell, eager to take him for a ride. In her haste, she left her keys in the car.
>
> As Kathy and Rick ran back down the stairs a few minutes later, they watched in horror as Kathy's Firebird disappeared around the corner, driven by its "new" owner.

Here are some precautions you can take that will make your car less likely to be broken into or stolen:

- No matter how short the errand, never leave your keys in your car or leave the engine running when you get out of your car—even in your own driveway. Many amateur thieves watch for unattended cars whose engines are running. The more time-consuming you make it to steal your car, the more likely a thief will try his luck on someone else's vehicle.

- Don't park at the end of a block if you can help it. Park with the front wheels turned sharply into the curb and apply your emergency brake. If you have front wheel drive, when you park place your vehicle in "park" and apply the emergency brake. If you have a stick shift, put the car in "forward" or "reverse" and apply the emergency brake. All four wheels will be locked. All these tactics make it hard for thieves to tow your car away.

- Park only in well-lighted areas and avoid deserted streets, if possible.

- Place all packages and valuables out of sight. (That means in the trunk or under the seats, not on the seat covered with a coat or blanket.)

- Don't transfer luggage, packages or other valuables to your trunk after you park your car. Pack your trunk *before* you reach a parking place so thieves can't tell what's inside it.

- In your driveway, park your car with the nose toward the street so that anyone tampering with the engine can be seen more easily.

- Remove your car radio each time you park in a "high risk" neighborhood. Placing a decal or hand made sign that says "No Radio" in the car window saves the thief the trouble of breaking in and saves you the trouble of replacing a car lock or shattered window.

- Replace standard door lock buttons with the slim, tapered kind. They're almost impossible to pull up with a coat hanger.

IT ONLY TAKES A MOMENT

Stolen radios or packages are a nuisance, and may be costly losses—but they can't compare to the threat to human life that you may face.

"It was Friday night, the end of an exhausting work week, and I was having dinner guests on Saturday," Dana said.

"I decided to do my food shopping after work so I could spend Saturday cooking and cleaning. So I parked my car and dashed into the supermarket, hoping to pick up the few things I needed and get out as fast as possible.

"The store was jammed with people waiting in line and my nerves were frayed. Yet somehow I managed to be out in less than twenty minutes.

"On the way home I realized I needed gas, so I pulled into the station, told the guy to fill 'er up and handed him my charge card," Dana explained.

"A minute later he walked back to my car and said, 'I'm sorry, but this card won't go through. Please come to the office with me.'

"Well, I was furious. I told him there was no reason for my card not to go through—there wasn't an outstanding balance, or anything.

"I got out of the car and walked with him to the office," she said, remembering what happened next.

"As soon as I stepped inside he closed the door and said, 'Lady, you have a big problem.' My heart started pounding as I wondered what he was talking about.

"He handed my card back to me and said, 'There's nothing wrong with your credit card. There's a man in the back seat of your car, and I couldn't think of any other way of getting you out of there. I'm sorry if I frightened you.'

"Frightened me? That was the understatement of the year. I couldn't believe what he was saying! Then I thought back and remembered how I had planned to just run in and out of the grocery store and hadn't bothered to lock my doors. I didn't expect to be gone that long.

"The service station attendant called the police and they came and took the guy out of my car. I realize I was very lucky. I hate to think what might have happened that night if I hadn't stopped for gas."

3000 Pounds of Protection

This story graphically illustrates just one way criminals can get into your car. But there are others.

What's your first reaction when, at a red light or stop sign, a driver bumps into your car? No serious damage, but enough to get your attention. If you're like most people, your first reaction is to jump out of the car and check the damage. Learn to wait a few seconds before you do.

Take a look around. Are you in a well-traveled area? Is it night? Are there other people around who could help if you ran into trouble? Who is the driver of the other car? Is it a man—is he alone or with other passengers? These are some of the things you must consider *before* you jump out of your car.

If you are involved in such a situation and do not feel comfortable about getting out of your car, get as much information as you can about the other car by looking through your rear-view mirror. Or stay in your car and have the other driver come to you. With your doors locked, roll your window down just enough to exchange the necessary information. Then drive to the nearest police station, or call in the incident as soon as you can. Explain the situation and your reason for leaving the scene of the accident. The police will advise you further.

If you must get out of your vehicle, consider these possibilities. Be aware of the man who looks for a woman driving alone, especially at night. When the victim's car comes to a stop, he taps his car into her bumper, knowing the woman will jump right out of the car, making herself vulnerable. Many incidents have occurred when a woman has gotten out to check the damage with the other driver, and a passenger from the offending car sneaked up and snatched her handbag off the front seat.

If someone tries to force his way into your car, keep your hand on the horn to attract attention—the last thing any criminal wants. Be aware of where you are. In a desolate parking area or side road, blaring your horn may go unnoticed. In that case, put your car in gear and drive away quickly. If your car is disabled and you can't drive off, be prepared to get away on foot if someone forcibly tries to get inside your car.

Whichever side he is trying to get in, move over to the other side in anticipation of fleeing from your vehicle. Formulate an evacuation plan. If you have to run, know where you'll be running to. Otherwise, you might find yourself at a dead end with no way out.

If your breakdown is just from a flat tire, put your car in gear and drive to the nearest, safest place and seek help. You'll probably ruin the wheel, but that's inconsequential when your life is at stake.

Also, if your car does break down and someone offers to take you to a gas station, whether it's just one person or a family of seven, simply say "No, thank you," and ask them to call the police for you. That's a safer option than taking a chance with a stranger.

PARKING LOTS AND GARAGES

If you're a frequent driver, you know the problems and frustrations of trying to find a (legitimate) place to park. Whether you're trying to find a space on a crowded city street or you're looking for a close-to-the-entrance spot at the mall, it's hard to avoid the hassle of parking. And attended parking lots and garages present their own set of problems.

When you park in a parking lot, the attendant only needs to have your ignition key—not your house keys, the spare set of keys to your roommate's car, the trunk key, your office keys, etc.

And he doesn't need to know exactly how long you'll be gone. That's none of his business. If you believe he needs this information so he won't have to shuffle cars around, you're forgetting something very important. He gets paid to park and juggle a lot full of cars. That's why he asked you for your key in the first place. Give an indefinite answer, such as "I'm not sure" or "Not long." If pressed further, say "As long as it takes."

Here are some suggestions to help you prevent having your car go on a joy ride with a car thief at the wheel:

- Before you leave the car, reset your trip odometer to zero, or jot down the mileage on a piece of paper. When you return, check the mileage. There's no excuse for your car being moved more than a few tenths of a mile.

- When you return to your car, if you believe your car has been out sightseeing without you, *do not* approach the attendant. Instead, walk to the nearest pay phone and call the police. Explain the extra mileage and say you're concerned that your car may have been taken off the lot without your permission. They will tell you what to do.

- As important as it is to check your mileage when you return to your car, checking your license plate to make sure it's yours is just as critical. Sometimes criminals will steal license plates from "clean" cars and put them on stolen ones, then go and commit a crime or two. Afterwards, when an astute witness tells the police they got the license plate number of the get-away car, guess who the police come looking for? If you don't know your license plate number, make it a point to learn it immediately.

BUYING A USED CAR

You need to buy a car, but have a limited budget. A friend tells you about a used car dealer who guarantees that no one sells cars cheaper than he does. Should you buy from a place like this? And if you do, how can you be sure you are not buying a "hot" car?

A vehicle, in most cases, is the second largest purchase you make, next to a home. So, buy with care. If you knowingly buy a stolen car, you can be arrested. If you unwittingly buy a stolen car, you could lose the car and your money.

Keep these tips in mind:

- Buy your car from a reputable, licensed dealer who has been in business for many years. Be wary of deals that sound "too good to be true."
- When buying from a private individual, be suspicious of a seller with no fixed address, place of employment or phone number.
- Ask the seller for information about the past financing and insurance on the vehicle. Verify the information with the bank, finance company or agent.
- Check the VIN (Vehicle Identification Number) on the car for alterations or replacement. It must match the VIN on the title. If the VIN plate is missing rivets, is scratched or bent, you should suspect tampering.
- Thieves often remove the VIN plate and replace it with one from a wrecked vehicle. If in doubt about the plate's authenticity, have the vehicle checked by a new car dealer who handles the same model. Or, contact a law enforcement agency.

- Be suspicious of a fresh paint job on a newer model. It may indicate cover-up work to change the car's identity.
- Check the license plate and any inspection or emission stickers to be sure they are current and were issued by the correct state.
- Obtain at least one set of original manufacturer's keys. Be suspicious if the seller provides you with only re-made keys if you are buying a late-model car.
- Complete all paperwork (including transfer of title, if applicable) at the time of sale with both parties present.

SELLING YOUR CAR

It's time to buy a car, but you need to sell the one you already have. You know you could go to the dealership where you will be buying your new car and use it as a trade-in, but feel you could get more money if you sold it on your own.

You place an ad in the classified section of your local newspaper and wait for the calls to start pouring in. What's wrong with that? Nothing, until someone comes to take your old car out for a test drive.

"This well-dressed young man came to my door and said he was the one who called about my car," Rachel explained to the detective.

"He came an hour earlier than he was supposed to and my husband hadn't come home from work. He apologized for the mix-up in the schedule. He said his plans had changed and hoped I wouldn't mind showing him the car right then.

"He asked questions about the battery, the tires and the engine. I just didn't know what to say. I did tell him that my husband would be home soon, and that if he could come back, I was sure Bill could answer his questions. Instead, he said he wanted to drive the car around the neighborhood a bit to see how it drove.

"What could I do? I felt terrible that I couldn't answer his questions and he did seem to be in such a hurry, so I gave him my keys. He promised me he'd be right back," Rachel sobbed.

"Not only did he steal my car, but also my key ring, which had the keys to my house, the garage and Bill's car on it."

Rachel and her husband could have traded her car to a dealer or found a reputable gas station that would try to sell the car for them. They preferred doing it themselves. If you were Rachel, what would you have done in the same situation?

A. Asked to hold the man's wallet and car keys for security.

B. Asked for his watch or some type of collateral.

C. Gone with him.

D. Packed a snack, rounded up the neighbors and all gone for a test drive.

E. Told him you'd already sold the car.

If you chose "A," what would you expect to find in his wallet that would reassure you he would return your car? Lots of money? Not likely. Asking for his car keys could mean that you'd then have a set of keys for a car that was worthless or stolen.

If "B" was your answer, regardless of the type of car you were selling and the type of watch he was wearing, most likely he would still have gotten the better deal.

If "C" caught your eye, I hope that's all it caught, because this answer is the one that would put you in the greatest jeopardy. Remember, this person is a *stranger*.

"D" has possibilities. After all, there's safety in numbers. That's the key—numbers. You'd have a better chance with at least two other people with you (seat them in the back) than with only one person.

This answer also applies if you are answering an ad to buy a car. Remember, you, too, would want to test drive any car you were thinking of buying. Bring at least two other people with you. If you can only get one person—a female—to go with you, then have her sit in the back seat directly behind the driver and you sit up front. If a man is coming with you, have him sit up front in the passenger seat and you sit in the back behind the driver.

What if you can't find anyone to go with you? Reschedule your appointment for another time. Yes, you might lose the car of your dreams, but that's a small price to pay for what you could lose.

As you know by now, "E"—lose the sale—is the best answer. Of course, it's easier said than done, especially if buying your new car depends upon the immediate sale of your old one. But after reviewing the other possibilities, you have to admit this answer is the one that makes the most safety sense.

And if you do decide against selling the car to someone, for whatever reason, you don't need to give the prospective buyer any excuses. If you do, he'll ask: "When did you sell it? I just called you fifteen minutes ago." "How much did you sell it for?" "So why is it still in your driveway?" A simple explanation such as "The car has been sold" is all that is necessary to give anyone.

Chapter 4

❖❖❖❖❖

Rape

No crime engenders more emotion and confusion than rape. Ask ten people to define rape and you'll get ten different definitions. And men and women are equally confused about the subject.

What Is Rape?

Rape is *not* a sexual crime, but a crime of violence. The motive is not primarily to have sex, but to establish power and humiliate the victim by using physical force, threat or intimidation. It can include any form of penetration: oral, anal or vaginal.

FBI statistics say that approximately one in ten women is raped during her lifetime. These statistics are based on the number of rapes reported across the country, but because rape is one of the least reported crimes, law enforcement officials estimate that the number of actual rapes is many times higher than the number reported.

Facts and Fiction

How accurate are your perceptions about rape? Take this true-false quiz to find out:
1. Rape is almost exclusively an inner-city phenomenon.
2. Rapists are usually men who are deprived of sexual relations.
3. If no weapon or actual physical violence was used, a
   woman cannot bring charges of rape.

4. Women who hitchhike or go to singles bars are asking to be raped.
5. Many rapes could be eliminated if women would not dress seductively.
6. Testimony about a woman's past sexual conduct is important evidence in a rape trial.

All of the above statements are false. And the biggest myth of all is "It can't happen to me." The fact is, it can happen to *anyone*. By insisting that it can't happen to you, you are increasing the chances that it will. Ignorance makes you a more likely victim.

Who Is the Rapist

Who commits these acts of violence? Let's take a look at the rapist.

Of course, we tend to think of rape as a random crime committed by a deranged stranger. But surprisingly, more than one-third of all rapes are committed by someone the victim knows (acquaintance or date rape), making the crime even more heinous.

It can be anyone—a family member, neighbor, co-worker, boss, boyfriend, clergyman, doctor or even one's husband. It's impossible to spot a rapist in a crowd; he looks just like any other man. Many are pillars of respectability in their communities and it's under the guise of respectability that they often commit and get away with their crimes.

The Victim

Often the act of rape is planned ahead. The potential rapist looks for a victim who is vulnerable to attack. Some rapists look for victims who are handicapped or who can't react appropriately or swiftly to the threat of rape. They may choose isolated areas such as remote sections of parks or deserted streets as settings for their attacks.

Other assailants look for environments that are easily entered and relatively safe. They make certain that the victim is alone and that they will not be interrupted.

Older homes, converted into apartments or condos, are the easiest residences for a rapist to get into. Basement or first-floor apartments are especially tempting. Isolated areas, such as remote sections of parks or deserted streets are other likely places where women may be accosted.

Apartments with doormen or security guards are the most difficult residences for the rapist to enter.

Some people believe that a woman is asking to be raped because she dresses or walks in a certain way, but that is like saying that a bank is asking to be robbed because there is money in it or that a man is asking to be mugged because he is carrying a wallet.

Quite often, rapists are repeat offenders, and many were abused themselves when they were children. These people act out the same violent behaviors that they were subjected to, rather than getting the vital help needed to break the cycle of inflicting pain on others.

DATE RAPE

A particularly insidious type of rape has been brought to the public's attention recently—date rape (or acquaintance rape). That's when someone you have agreed to go out with turns the date into your worst nightmare.

"We met at a singles party and hit it off right away," Melissa recalled. "I was with my girlfriend and Roger offered us both a ride home. We dropped Carla off first and then I gave Roger directions to my house, which was only a mile or so away. He said his apartment was on the way and he wanted to check his answering machine. He said he was waiting for a message from an important client that would make or break the next day's sales presentation. So I said sure we could stop at his place first, but that I didn't want to go upstairs.

"We stopped in front of his apartment building, which by the way, wasn't close by, and I said I would wait for him in the car. He said, 'What's the matter, don't you trust me?'

"I thought I was hurting his feelings, so I went with him up to his place. Well, you can probably guess the rest. He started pulling at my clothes the minute he closed the door and he pushed me onto the couch. In spite of my screams and my attempts to fight him off, he raped me.

"When it was over, he threw $5.00 at me and told me to take a cab home. He also said that if I told anyone, they wouldn't believe me because everyone who knew him thought he was a great guy.

"I got out of there as fast as I could, hailed the first cab I could find and cried all the way home.

"When I got back to my apartment my roommate was still awake and I couldn't hide my hysteria from her. I expected her to be totally supportive, but instead she told me to forget about reporting the rape to the police. She said that Roger's father was a bigwig at a huge company and that nothing would ever come of my accusation.

"So I took a long hot shower, threw away the clothes I had been wearing that night and tried to forget what happened. Of course, I haven't been able to. I think about it all the time. It upsets me so much to know that he's probably doing the same thing to other women and won't be caught until someone has enough guts to file a complaint and see it through. I wish now that I had been the one to do it."

Here are some things you can do to lessen the chances of date rape:

Remove the opportunity. This is the most effective technique. As we discuss in Chapter 1, if there is no opportunity, there can be no crime.

If you meet a man and wish to see him again, take *his* phone number. Give *him* a call. If you can't bring yourself to do that, have him call you at work. If you don't work or you work at home, give him your phone number, but not your address or last name.

If you choose to see a "new" man again, meet him at a coffee shop, deli, or cafe—someplace where there are a lot of people. Forget those intimate, out of the way places. You don't know this guy, remember? Stick to populated places for awhile.

During your second get together, you can decide if you wish to see the person again. If you don't, you can glance at your watch, tell him you're running late, and leave. If he calls again, be honest (yes, easier said than done) and say you'd rather not get together again. You know he's going to press you further. Think about your answer and don't allow him to bully you. Be firm. And if he persists, hang up the phone. (This is when you'll be glad you didn't give out your last name or address right away.)

Make your meaning clear. Learn how to put a quick stop to behavior that you find unacceptable by firmly saying "No" when that's what you mean, and be sure that your body language is giving the same message. Don't give confusing signals which might be perceived as acquiescence, only to have to stop a man's advances later on.

Watch out for bad guys. Avoid men who show little respect for women, use vulgar language, and take physical liberties such as forcing kisses and rough hugging. Also, be aware of men with short tempers who slap faces and twist arms.

Avoid drugs and alcohol. A large percentage of date (or acquaintance) rapes occur in someone's home or apartment, and usually there has been some drinking or use of drugs. If you go back to your date's place or bring him back to yours, and you partake of alcohol or drugs with him, you are definitely at risk.

Your Best Defense

What should you do if you think someone is about to rape you? Other than trying to talk your way out of it ("I have my period," "I have AIDS," "I'm going to throw up," or any other statement that might work), the choices you have—to protect your life—are to offer no resistance, and hope for an opportunity to escape or to be as aggressive as possible (providing your assailant is unarmed), disabling him enough to ensure your safety.

If you were to find yourself in this situation, what would you do? You need to plan today—not tomorrow—for your safety and personal well-being.

Take a few minutes right now to imagine how you would react. What *would* you do? Would you be passive and not fight back, no matter what? Or would you resist with everything you had?

If you would choose to be passive, that's okay. Don't think that means there's something wrong with you. Being passive can mean something as simple as pretending to be asleep if an intruder enters your bedroom, hoping he will leave without a confrontation.

Being passive is not the same as "giving in." It may be the most courageous decision on your part not to endanger yourself any more than is necessary. If you know that you would be incapable of physically fighting back, then don't. And don't listen to people who insist you should fight back, no matter what. Because if you attempt to do something that isn't right for you, you could be placing yourself in an even more dangerous position.

If you are not able to strike effectively or with enough force, a half-hearted attempt at self-defense could anger your assailant and might even get you killed. You know yourself best. Do what you have to do to stay alive—even if that means doing nothing.

Wait it out. There may come a time when he puts down his weapon or is distracted long enough so that you can flee to safety.

If you *are* determined to fight back, make sure your assailant is unarmed. Unless you are specifically trained in the martial arts, don't even attempt to disarm a knife-wielding or gun-toting opponent.

Should you choose to fight off your attacker, you'll only have a few precious seconds to do so and only one chance to get it right. You must give it your very best shot, as hard and as forcefully as you can—to the most vulnerable areas of his body (eyes, nose, ears, temple, windpipe, etc.). See Chapter 5 for specific areas to target.

There are no retakes, no second chances to get it right, no changing to another tactic halfway through a move because you just thought of a more effective technique. That's why rehearsing mentally is so important.

To fight or not to fight? The answer depends on the situation and on you—your personality and capabilities. When it comes to protecting your life, anything and everything goes. There are no rules—only those which you impose upon yourself. Run through different scenarios in your mind, so if you are ever faced with a physical threat, your response will be automatic.

IF YOU ARE RAPED

Since rape is not a federal offense, the laws and procedures for filing suit vary from state to state. For example, some states acknowledge marital rape while others do not. That's why it's so important for victims to contact their local law enforcement agency or their local rape crisis clinic for assistance.

If you are raped, there are some things you must do and some you *must not*. First, you need to decide immediately whether or not you will report the rape to the police and follow the prosecution through the court system. Remember, if you choose not to file a complaint against the rapist, you are giving him tacit permission to rape another woman.

If you decide not to report the rape immediately, and change your mind at a future time, you may have missed the opportunity to provide the evidence necessary to prosecute the rapist effectively. If you *do* decide to report the rape:

1. *Do not* eat, drink, shower or brush your teeth—you could be destroying valuable evidence.

2. Protect the clothes you were wearing at the time of the rape by carefully folding them and putting them in a paper (not plastic) bag.

3. Go to the nearest hospital for an exam. Hospitals are equipped with kits for rape victims so they can take samples from your vaginal area as well as scrapings under your fingernails for fibers, tissue, hair, etc., that you might have come in contact with. The hospital or police department will keep this as evidence for 6 to 12 months

4. Report the crime to the nearest police station. Try to provide the most specific information and description of your assail-

ant. Even if you were blindfolded, or could not see the rapist, the crime may fit the pattern of known rapists or of other reported rapes in the area.

You may choose to speak to a female officer if that would make you more comfortable. However, male law enforcement personnel are also trained in rape crisis intervention and can assist you if a female officer is not available.

Or you may decide to go to a rape crisis clinic first to speak with a counselor who will advise you of what further steps you need to take. Often they will provide a victim's advocate who will guide you through the complicated judicial system.

They will also be there for you if you choose to tell your family of the rape. And they will offer counseling, often by someone who is also a rape victim. There are numerous hotlines and rape crisis clinics throughout the country. They are as close as your nearest telephone. If your city or town telephone directory does not list a rape crisis center, ask the operator for the one nearest you.

THE AFTERMATH

Many women are permanently scarred, physically and psychologically, as a result of being raped. It can take several months, years or a lifetime for a victim of rape to go through what psychologists refer to as "Rape Trauma Syndrome"—the aftereffects of the violent crime.

In addition to the victim needing counseling, the victim's family (parents, husband or special man in her life, especially) should also receive counseling to help them understand what the victim is going through and how to better help her. Many relationships have disintegrated because a husband or boyfriend could not understand or cope with the rape.

Rape is the most intimate of crimes. It is so personal, in fact, that it often causes its victim to question even reporting it. But if we hope to keep rapists from being repeat offenders and to deter them from committing this horrible crime, we need to report, prosecute and punish all rapists fully.

By doing so, we can end the "stigma of rape" and expose rape for what it is—a violent, *non*-sexually-motivated crime, perpetrated by an assailant who needs psychological counseling as well as removal from society.

Chapter 5

❖❖❖❖❖❖

Fighting
Back

For many women, crime stories in the news, those we hear from friends and neighbors, and our own everyday experiences cause us to be fearful.

We may feel a surge of adrenaline when we unlock the front door and step into a darkened home. Or experience tension as we walk through an underground parking garage, or a skipped heartbeat when we answer the phone and someone hangs up on the other end.

For some women, particularly seniors, this fear translates into reorganizing their lives so that more and more activities are scheduled during daylight hours rather than after dark. Many women simply refuse to go out in the evening, whether it's to visit friends, go to a movie or concert or to shop, unless they have someone accompanying them.

When we experience this type of fear, we are likely to limit our participating in a fulfilling life. Many of us protect ourselves from the daily threats to our safety by avoiding activities and missing opportunities.

THREATENING SITUATIONS

We are faced with a dilemma. Should we go along ignoring potential dangers, hoping that we will be lucky enough to avoid confrontations? Should we restrict our lives as a form of self-protection, narrowing our options to limit possible exposure to harm? Or should we reject the restrictions and arm ourselves or study self-defense and plan strategies for dealing with the adversities?

Certainly, ignoring the dangers will not make them go away, and hiding

❖

behind locked doors greatly reduces the quality of life. In addition to learning how not to be selected a victim, as covered in Chapter 1, here are some other options.

CARRYING A GUN

Anyone who considers carrying a gun must deal with moral as well as legal issues. Law enforcement officials do not advocate carrying a handgun on the street. In some places it is illegal; in most cases, it's just not smart.

Think about the following situations and consider the possible consequences. If you fire your handgun outside your home, even if you have a permit to carry the gun, it could cause you serious legal repercussions.

Ask yourself this: If I were confronted by a criminal, could I—would I—without hesitation, pull the trigger and shoot my assailant? This is the *most important question* you must answer *before* heading down to your local police department for a permit to carry or to purchase a weapon. If you could not with all certainty answer "yes" to this question, then reconsider carrying a gun for protection.

If you think that having a gun in your purse would give you confidence—that in the face of trouble, you would pull out your gun, wave it at your assailant and watch him run away scared—you're not being realistic. In actuality, he might take the gun away and might even use it on *you.*

Were you to panic with a gun in your hand, you could shoot the wrong person or kill an unarmed robber. The result could be prosecution, a civil lawsuit for damages or, at the very least, a lifetime of regret.

If you carry a gun in your purse and your handbag is stolen, you will have armed another criminal.

SELF-DEFENSE SPRAYS AND ALARMS

Instead of carrying a gun, consider a self-defense spray. States differ in their requirements for the purchase and use of these products. It is important that you check with your local law enforcement agency concerning the laws in your state.

These substances come in pocket-sized dispensers and home-sized canisters. There are two types of tear gas. CN gas (better known as mace) causes sharp burning of the skin and mucous membranes in 3 to 10 seconds when sprayed in the face. However, people who are under the influence of alcohol or drugs will not be affected by CN tear gas because it acts on the nerve centers which are not receptive to pain at that time. The same shortcoming is true for CS gas which, although it is stronger than CN, takes between 45 and 60 seconds to take effect.

Another option is to use a derivative of hot red cayenne peppers (capsicum), which uses a different principle than tear gas. Rather than acting as an irritant, it produces inflammation of the mucous membranes. It is this difference which enables it to be effective on even those who don't feel pain, such as psychotics, drunks and drug abusers.

If you do decide to carry a self-defense spray, it is important to be sure that you buy it from a reputable source, not on the street. Check the expiration date regularly (if using non-capsicum sprays), replace your supply annually and practice using it. Keep your spray in an accessible place where it can be grabbed and used quickly. Remember to unlock the safety latch. Keep the nozzle away from you and keep on the move after you spray it, so you won't be affected by the gas. Note that tear gas sprays may not be carried on airplanes.

On the street, keep the container of spray in your hand—not in your purse. How many of us can find and retrieve anything from our purses in the time we would have available to release the latch, aim and spray an attacker? As with any weapon you carry, know that this one, too, can be taken from you and used against you. It can also incite your attacker to more violence.

You can give yourself a degree of security if you carry some form of personal alarm, which can serve two purposes. If you use it at the appropriate time, it may cause a prospective attacker to turn on his heels. And, hopefully, it will also attract the attention of people nearby who could come to your aid. These devices take the form of whistles or shrill, battery operated "sirens." See the appendix for sources of items mentioned in this section.

Physical Self-Defense

Street weapons can be risky forms of self-defense. There is no way to ensure that the criminal won't have mace himself or a bigger gun or longer knife. Don't allow a false sense of security to go along with your can of self-defense spray. It's better to have a sense of street smarts and some self-defense than to rely on a spray or a gun.

Some type of self-defense training is a good idea. You don't need to go all the way up to a black belt; what you're aiming for is a good dose of self-confidence. That's something you can use in any situation.

Self-defense courses are given at many universities, YM and YWCA's and at some rape crisis centers.

If you should decide to enroll in self-defense class, make sure it is co-ed. You need to work out with a male partner so you become accustomed to feeling a man's strength and grip in various choke and hold techniques. This will also help you gauge the height difference when practicing certain self-defense moves such as an open-hand blow to the nose, neck or chin.

Learn the pressure points or nerve centers of the body which are particularly vulnerable to blows from your hand or foot. Knowing a few pressure points and having the self-confidence to execute some self-defense techniques could give you the edge in deflecting an attack. Concentrate your strength and energy on hitting one or two of these areas instead of beating your fists against your attacker's arm or chest:

Nose. A simple upward thrust of the palm to the nose will cause intense pain and watering eyes.

Ears. A moderate blow causes pain; a heavier blow could burst an eardrum.

Eyes. If you're close enough, stick a finger or two or any object into your assailant's eyes. If he is wearing glasses, use your thumbs or forefingers and thrust them up under the glasses directly into the eyes.

Solar Plexus. A blow to this fleshy area (just below where the ribs part) with an elbow or fist can immobilize your assailant long enough for you to escape.

Groin. Never aim for this area first. It's the first place your attacker will protect. Choose another less protected area for your initial attack.

Shin. Aim for this area whenever possible. Because the extensive concentration of nerves in this area is unprotected by muscle, a quick kick here is extremely painful.

Instep. A hard stomp here with your heel causes pain and can shatter the small bones in the arch of the foot.

Fingers. If you are restrained, take hold of the little finger(s) and pull back as hard and as fast as you can.

Conserve your energy. Don't waste it. You don't need to be an Amazon, just use your power to its best advantage. The strength you now possess is more than adequate. Learning the techniques can be helpful. But the big payoff comes from the confidence you build—knowing that you *can* take charge— that you are not helpless after all.

More Power . . .
At
Home

Chapter 6

❖❖❖❖❖❖

Beating
the Burglars

According to the FBI, in 1990 a burglary occurred every 10 seconds; two out of three burglaries were residential. That adds up to more than 3 million burglaries reported in 1990, resulting in 3.5 billion dollars in total loss. An equal number of burglaries took place during the day as at night.

Is there anything you can do to avoid becoming another statistic? Yes, but first you must understand something about how a burglar chooses his target. Then you need to implement some simple (and not necessarily expensive) precautionary measures to make your home more secure and less likely to be victimized.

While a skilled burglar will always get into your house if he is really determined, the run-of-the-mill thief is not so single-minded. Tight security goes a long way in persuading the average burglar to try another home—one which offers easier pickings.

SECURING THE ENTRYWAYS

While no home can be completely burglar-proofed, you can reduce the chances of a break-in if you take certain precautions. The most obvious way to prevent unwanted intruders from entering your home is to secure all the entries.

Want to frustrate a burglar? Reduce or remove his opportunities for crime. Use simple, practical, preventive techniques to implement your security program.

Doors. All outside doors ideally should be solid-core construction, or metal clad. Hollow-core wooden doors are easily kicked or battered in.

All door frames should be solid in construction and firmly attached to the house's structure. Street-facing hinges on your outer doors should be replaced with non-removable hinges (available at your local hardware store).

Install a wide-angle peephole, which allows you to see visitors without opening the door. And *never* rely on a chain lock as your only security device. To do so is almost as dangerous as leaving the door completely unlocked.

Door locks. All outside doors should have securely mounted deadbolts. Deadbolt locks can only be opened by a key or a thumb-turned knob. A double cylinder deadbolt must also have a key to open it when locked from the inside, and is particularly useful when there are glass panes in a door.

The deadbolt is used in conjunction with a wood frame-reinforcer which contains screws that go through the frame and into the studs, acting as a deterrent to kick-in attacks. Often, insurance companies will require that you have deadbolt locks as a condition to their providing homeowner's insurance.

Certain locks offer better protection than others from breaking and entering. Consult your local locksmith for his recommendations, or refer to the February 1990 issue of *Consumer Reports* on home security ("Locks and Alarms"), available at your library.

Inexpensive install-it-yourself locks can be purchased in a hardware store and, while they may not provide the optimum protection, can still serve as deterrents to break-ins.

Whichever locks you choose, remember: The more locks there are on a door, the longer it will take to get past them and the less likely your door will be chosen by a burglar.

Sliding doors. To prevent both panels of a sliding door from being lifted up and out of their tracks, secure the stationary panel with a screw that fastens from the inside through the door and frame. The top track should have small screws protruding down so the door barely clears them.

When locked, wedge the sliding door with a "Charley Bar," a metal rod that bars the door even if the lock is picked or broken. This can be purchased at a hardware store or locksmith's. A less desirable option is to wedge a wooden rod (a broomstick or a dowel, for example) in the bottom track.

Secure sliding doors with a sliding door lock or door alarm that shrieks when jostled. Or hang a wind chime in front of your patio doors. If an intruder enters your home, the chimes can alert you to possible danger in enough time for a safe escape.

Double-hung windows. These are the most common type of window, and easiest to jimmy open. To improve security, drill a slanted hole through the top of the bottom sash and into, but not all the way through, the bottom of the top sash. Insert a nail into this hole to prevent the opening of either sash, but make sure it can easily be removed from the inside in case the window needs to be used as a fire exit. Another option is a keyed window sash lock or a lock that mounts on top of the sash and can also be locked in a ventilating position. Be sure the key is kept in a nearby place in case of a fire.

Sliding windows. These should be secured in the same manner as sliding doors.

Jalousie (louvered) windows. These are impossible to secure without adding a protective grill, which is very expensive—and makes escape difficult in case of a fire. Consider replacing them entirely with another type of window.

Casement windows. In addition to being difficult to secure, they can be easily forced or pried open if the crank or push bar is loose. For a quick fix, remove the crank when not at home.

Basement windows. These come in a variety of sizes, shapes and types and most are difficult to make secure by adding hardware. The least expensive solution is to make it impossible for a body to fit through the windows' openings. This can be achieved by putting two bars on each window or by using a security grill, but be aware that doing so makes emergency exit impossible.

An alternative to securing basement windows is to have a strong door and secure lock on the entryway leading from the basement to the rest of the house so that even if someone gains entrance through the basement, he is denied access to the rest of your home.

Attic openings. In attached garages, carports and in some apartments or duplexes, attic openings should be viewed as points of entry for the burglar when the openings are accessible by folding ladder or stair. Install a padlock and case-hardened hasp with concealed screws for security. Your hardware store can supply these.

Window air conditioning units. While not conventional entryways, window units can be easily pushed in or pulled out of their mounts to make them so. Make sure they are attached securely to the window frames.

SECURITY ALARM SYSTEMS

If you feel you need more protection than door and window locks alone provide, a home security system may be what you need.

From surveillance cameras and infrared detectors to touch-tone code alarms and panic buttons, alarm systems can be purchased for a few hundred dollars to several thousand dollars. Before you make an investment, be sure you understand the degree of protection you need, then look for the system that will afford you this protection within your budget constraints.

While you don't need to over-alarm your home, be sure the system will do the job that needs to be done. Make sure that all exterior doors and accessible windows are considered for wiring.

The best alarm system is one that has battery back-up in case of power loss. The battery will need replacement approximately every four or five years, and periodic tests should be conducted to ensure that everything is in order.

Keep all wiring for the system inside the house. This prevents a burglar from cutting the security wires so he can enter your home undetected.

A wireless alarm system works off radio frequencies and has the disadvantage that interference can be caused by aircraft and garage door openers. It operates on a battery which requires replacement.

Whichever type of alarm system you consider, remember these points:

- Get written cost estimates, compare companies and check their reputations. (Recommendations from friends and neighbors are especially useful.)
- An effective alarm system should protect *all* points of entry into your home.
- Price is no guarantee of quality. Ask your local police department to help you determine which system meets your needs.
- Don't have decals on your doors or windows advertising the specific type of alarm system or company used. They may tip the burglar off about how to disarm the system. Use more generic warning decals, which are inexpensive to purchase. (You can use these even if you have no alarm system at all—they may be enough of a deterrent to keep an intruder from choosing your home.)

Important note: An alarm system is only as reliable as the person who remembers to activate it. And even the most elaborate system is rendered useless if you allow strangers into your home.

Additional Ways to Secure Your Home

Inexpensive door and window alarms. Powered by batteries, they are no larger than a small tape player. When a door or window is opened, these alarms produce a loud, piercing noise capable of waking even the soundest sleeper.

Installation is simple, using either two screws or double-backed adhesive strips, and can be accomplished in a matter of minutes.

Door stops. These can be plain or fancy. The fancy kind looks like a regular, 7" long door stop. If you put it behind your door when you go to bed and the door is opened, the alarm gives off a shrill, pulsating siren-alarm. A simple rubber doorstop placed under a locked door considerably strengthens even a flimsy door. Either of these is handy to take with you when you travel.

Motion sensor alarms. Similar to the battery-powered door and window alarms, these are activated by motion. Any movement within the sensor's field will cause the alarm to sound. Two good places to put them are in your garage or in a downstairs room that is unoccupied during sleeping hours. They do not require permanent installation and may be moved around as desired.

Motion sensor outdoor lights. These devices are electric powered, outdoor floodlights which turn on automatically when motion is detected, and provide excellent lighting for porches and driveways. Most brands have a wide-angle sensor field that is adjustable for distances of 10-80 feet from the light fixture.

Installation does require removal of your existing outdoor fixture, and although they are easy to install (3 wires to connect), it might be wise to have an electrician do it for you.

Light-activated on/off switches. Easily installed, they can be used with your existing outdoor light fixture. They automatically turn lights on at sunset and off at sunrise.

On/off timers. These inexpensive units are excellent for turning interior lights, radios, televisions and stereos, on and off at pre-programmed intervals. They give your home the appearance of inside activity when you are away.

Wireless intercom. A relatively inexpensive device, this can be very effective if you live in an apartment. Find a neighbor whose schedule is similar to yours so you can alert each other to emergencies or problems.

A quick trip to your local hardware, electronics or discount store and a survey of the catalogs listed in the appendix will reveal these and other inexpensive security devices. While they don't have the flashing lights and other gadgetry of the home security systems costing hundreds or thousands of dollars, they can act as deterrents to forcible entry or give you sufficient warning to telephone the police for help.

THE WARM, FUZZY SECURITY SYSTEM

A survey was made of prison inmates who were serving time for breaking and entering. They were asked to rate various types of deterrents to burglary, in terms of which were most likely to keep them from trying to enter a home. The security system which came out on top was a dog!

A dog that barks when someone is at your door or when it hears the slightest noise can be the best protection you can have for your home. (It's also more fun than an expensive alarm system.) And having a dog around can give you a feeling of security that few other measures can offer.

HOME SECURITY CHECKLIST

Now that you've done all you can to prevent a thief from getting into your house through doors or windows, consider the following questions in assessing your total home security plan:

- Are your house numbers visible by day and night from the street? In an emergency, police or firefighters should be able to locate your house easily.
- Are timers used when you're away for any extended period of time? They should be attached to lights, and a television or radio, and should be set to turn on during times when they would normally be in use.
  Do not leave your lights on during the day. This signals a burglar that you are not home and won't be home until after dark.
- Does each room have window blinds or shades? Are they securely drawn at night to protect your privacy?
- Do all your telephones have emergency phone numbers posted on or near them?
- Do only family members and trusted friends have keys that fit your locks? (Don't hide a spare key in an obvious place like over the door jamb, under a door mat or taped under the mailbox.)

- If you keep weapons in your home, are they stored in a safe location to prevent accidental discovery?
- Is there a complete inventory list of all property, with extra copies at your insurance company and in your safe deposit box?

If you live in an apartment, also check the following:

- Do main outer doors lock automatically and do they require resident keys to open them?
- Does management re-key locks when you first move in or after a break-in? (If not, it's worth the cost of doing it yourself.)
- Are all stairways, hallways and surrounding areas well lit?
- Is the laundry room well lighted and safe from intruders?
- Does your building have a working emergency fire alarm? Do you know the location of the fire exits?

Read the Pre-vacation checklist in Chapter 15 for suggestions on how to protect your home when you're away for an extended period.

HIDING YOUR VALUABLES

A safe deposit box in the bank surely provides more protection for valuables than any "at home" substitute. But there are some ways to hide small items, such as jewelry, with relative security if you prefer to have them where you can get to them easily. (This is not recommended for items that have great value.)

- If you have a drop-down ceiling in any room in your home, place your valuable items in a pouch and stash them above one of the paneled sections.
- If your toilet is the tank-type, seal the items you wish to hide inside an air-tight plastic bag and suspend the bag inside the tank.
- A wall safe that can be recessed between wall studs can be concealed behind a painting or in a closet.
- A "book safe" which looks just like a novel when it sits on your shelf, actually opens to reveal a hiding place

for jewelry. And "safe cans" also look like the real thing. They can be aerosol, soda or food cans that anyone might have in their home. Unscrew the bottoms and you have small safes to stash your valuables.

Where feasible, it's a good idea to mark valuables with an identification number. A special code (phone number, driver's license number, etc.) can be etched with an engraving tool or with an invisible marking technique such as an ultraviolet pen, which reveals the marking when placed under ultraviolet light.

Burglars shy away from marked property because it can be quickly traced. Most police departments will help you mark your valuables and provide warning stickers for you to apply to your front and back doors and windows.

If you do leave valuable items at home or in your car or hotel room, don't stash them in obvious places—under the mattress, in your underwear drawer, or in the bottom of a laundry basket.

The danger in hiding your valuables is that you hide them so well that you cannot remember where you put them. Take measures to ensure that this does not happen to you! Tell a relative or close friend where you have hidden things or, even better, make note of your hiding places and keep the list in your safe deposit box.

Chapter 7

❖❖❖❖❖❖

Neighborhood Crime Watch

The most effective way to reduce crime in your neighborhood is to organize neighbors to help one another. Some neighborhoods have obvious crime problems and in others the crime is less apparent. But no matter where you live, don't make the mistake of believing that you live in a crime-free area. There is no such thing.

Crime feeds on apathy. If each of us simply minds her own business, our entire neighborhood is vulnerable. (With so many crimes being committed in front of people who don't even call the police, is it any wonder that crime rates are increasing?)

Alert neighbors, however, can change this trend by working with each other and the police to become aware of what is happening in their own neighborhoods. Community concern, alertness to suspicious activity and a willingness to cooperate with the police all contribute toward discouraging criminals.

Private Eyes

Do you know who your neighbors are and what goes on in your neighborhood, or are you oblivious to what goes on around you? Do you feel that if a problem doesn't affect you directly, you don't need to be concerned about it? If you choose to bury your head in the sand, sooner or later the problem will affect you, and probably when you least expect it.

You go away for a few days or come home late from work, only to find your home has been broken into and ransacked. The neighborhood's problem is now your problem—one that could have been prevented if you had taken part in a neighborhood crime watch program.

Get to know your neighbors and become familiar with their routines. You're going to become partners in watching the activities on your street or in your apartment house. Is it worth the investment? Most definitely!

STARTING A PROGRAM

The police need your help, your eyes and your ears. Most criminals choose not to operate in areas where the neighbors are alert.

- Arrange a neighborhood meeting to identify and discuss local problems.
- Recruit members of your neighborhood to attend the meeting.
- Form a leadership committee and select block or building captains.
- Plan neighborhood meetings with police officers assigned to your area.
- Don't hesitate to ask for help from the police. They will give professional advice to your watch group on what to look for, how to describe what is seen, how best to report incidents to the police and what steps can be taken to prevent crime in your neighborhood.
- Make a list of immediate neighbors' phone numbers. Also make a list of other watch members and leaders for reference. The neighborhood watch captain, her committee and the police should receive copies of this list. Be sure that permission is received from your neighbors *prior* to distributing this information to other members.
- Make sure all members are really residents of the neighborhood!
- Attend regular meetings with neighbors to monitor crime and problem areas in your neighborhood.
- Feel free to discuss the new program with people in your town or city. Word of mouth that such a program

has been started in your area should help keep criminals away.

The primary function of the neighborhood crime watch network is to observe and report to the police any suspicious or illegal activity. Don't take chances or try be a hero. And don't take the law into your own hands! Be a concerned neighbor and let common sense guide you.

Ten Steps to A Safer Neighborhood

1. Know your neighbors.
2. Assist your neighbors by watching their property.
3. Ask your neighbors to watch your property.
4. Get to know your local police officers.
5. Learn what information the police will need if you need to contact them about a crime or suspicious activity.
6. Be alert. If your dog is barking, check to see why! If someone screams, try to find out why! (Don't take action, just determine if there is a possible problem.)
7. Instruct your family on how to answer the door with safety in mind and how to respond to telephone calls. (See Children Home Alone, Chapter 11)
8. If you live near a school, establish rapport with school officials. Neighborhood problems that relate to their students can be dealt with cooperatively.
9. Report suspicious looking loiterers, salesmen, cars or activities. If something seems unusual to you, report it to the police.
10. Attend scheduled neighborhood meetings and keep informed of community problems and crime trends.

THE NEIGHBORHOOD MAP

Every neighborhood crime watch member should have a map of the neighborhood. Information should include each neighbor's name, address, phone number and what vehicles they own. Additional information such as their working hours, number of children, pets, and who's home during the day, helps in defining what is suspicious in your neighborhood.

Warning! Be sure you and your neighbors keep your maps in a safe place. Don't let strangers have a chance to obtain information about your neighborhood.

Chapter 8

❖❖❖❖❖❖

Uninvited
Guests

You've done your best to secure the entryways to your home and to keep criminals from selecting your house as a target. Now you need to know what to do in case someone *does* get past your security measures.

FACE-TO-FACE WITH A BURGLAR

Be alert as you approach your home. Have your house keys ready in your hand. If you notice something unusual or feel uneasy as you near your door, your intuitive alarm bell is ringing. *Do not open the door.* Of course, your first impulse is to rush in to see what was stolen and how much damage was done. But *think before you act!*

Get away from your house or apartment as quickly as possible. Burglars can have violent reactions if they are confronted while they are at work. Go to a neighbor's and call the police. Investigating is their job, not yours.

"It was an exceptionally frustrating day for me," Sarah began. The computer was down, my boss was upset because of the malfunction, the work was piling up on my desk, and all I could think of was how I could get out of work early. I needed to finish the shopping and do the cooking for my daughter's birthday party.

"I left my office a little early, did the food shopping and headed home.

"As I fumbled around in my bag for my house key, I remember feeling pretty satisfied with myself for organizing this party without Suzie having a clue. If I hadn't been so intent on patting myself on the back, I would have noticed how easily the front door opened. I dropped the grocery bags on the kitchen counter and went upstairs to change clothes.

"That's when I saw this guy with his back to me, rifling through my jewelry box. When he turned and faced me, I ran back down the stairs and out the front door as fast as I could. Fortunately, my next door neighbor had just come home and I rushed to use his phone to call the police.

"That night I celebrated more than Suzie's birthday. I celebrated my life—a life that might have ended if I hadn't been able to escape."

If, by some chance, you find yourself face-to-face with a burglar, do not confront him. *Don't* stand between him and his escape route, and *don't* demand that he turn over all your belongings or you'll call the police. Threatening a burglar is dangerous. Instead:

- Keep your head. If you're not being threatened with deadly force and can escape without crossing the burglar's path, do so immediately.
- Remain calm. If you are being threatened with a weapon, particularly a knife or a gun, do whatever you're told to do and nothing more.
- Don't waste time and precious energy by trying to bargain or reason with an intruder. Find out what he's after and assure him you'll give it to him.
- Keep "mugger money" available. That way you can give a thief what he wants and get him out quickly. (He usually wants to get out as badly as you want him to.)
- Once he is out of your home, call the police and give them a full description of the thief. Don't be intimidated into remaining silent.

AWAKENED BY AN INTRUDER

Something wakes you up. You lie quietly in bed trying to discover what it was that brought you back to wakefulness. That's when you realize that an intruder is prowling around your home. What should you do?

Pretending to sleep is the best reaction and perhaps the most difficult one, especially if the intruder is already in your bedroom, going through your purse or drawers. Remember, all a thief wants is to get in and out of your place with no interference from you. Most of the time an intruder is there looking for loot, not for confrontations. Refer also to Chapter 4, which deals with situations involving rape, in case robbery is not the motive.

Should You Keep a Gun in Your House?

There are approximately 200 million firearms in circulation in the United States; 60 to 70 million of them are handguns. Every year they are used to kill about 22,000 Americans.

Should you arm yourself? That's a critical personal choice. If you think you could use a handgun to keep from being robbed, ask yourself this question: Are you sure you would be willing to risk your life to keep from losing some replaceable property? See Chapter 5, which discusses self-defense.

If you do have a gun in your house you should be fully knowledgeable about its use and have a plan as to how you would use a firearm if the need should arise. Of even greater importance is that you be aware of the need to keep it safely out of the hands of children. People who purchase guns for protection should know that the chances are greater that the gun will be stolen, or used in a family suicide, accident or homicide than for its original purpose.

Handguns are prime targets for burglars. Every year more than 100,000 handguns are stolen from the homes of law-abiding citizens, according to Handgun Control, Inc., a national citizens organization for handgun policy. Many are later used in violent crimes by drug addicts, drug pushers and gang members.

Don't think for a moment that by showing a gun to an assailant, you guarantee he will be frightened away. If you pull a gun on someone as a defensive move, you'd better be prepared to fire it.

If you doubt whether you could pull the trigger and shoot someone, or use any other weapon (knife, baseball bat, tire iron) without hesitation, you should never pick up a weapon. You could turn an unarmed assailant who has no qualms about using violence into one who is armed—with your weapon.

Know the laws in your state regarding what is required to purchase, carry and discharge a gun, including what constitutes self-defense. Know what your rights are *before* you brandish a gun against an intruder in your home or a mugger on the street.

Chapter 9

✧✦✧✦✧✦✧

Troublemakers
at Your Door

Protecting the entries to your home can certainly give you a sense of security, but don't be lulled into believing that by doing so you have made your house impervious to criminal entry. If you believe that, you are overlooking the most obvious way anyone can gain entry to your home—by having an open invitation from you!

Once you open the door to a stranger, you have weakened your security; allow a stranger into your home, and you have rendered any security system useless.

Criminals have various ways of gaining access to your home or apartment. They're very creative and when one scam doesn't work, they'll try another.

TYPICAL PLOYS

In order to keep one step ahead of the bad guys, or at least keep up with them, you need to know some tricks of their trade—what they do and what they say to get you to open the door and let them into your home.

With that in mind, let's take a look at some of the ways criminals can gain access to your home, with you acting as their accomplice.

"A man came to the door dressed in a gas company shirt and cap and said he was there to read my meter," Emily explained.

"I told him that someone had come last week from the gas company and asked why they would send someone out again. He told me that there were reports of a gas leak in my neighborhood and all homes had to be checked.

"So I let him in and showed him to the basement door. That's when he turned on me with a gun in his hand, demanding my wedding ring and all the cash in the house. I gave him my ring and handed him my purse. I was so frightened, I just wanted him out of my house.

"As he was leaving, he threatened to kill me if I called the police. Once he was gone, I bolted the door and shook all over for nearly an hour. When I got the courage to walk to the phone, I dialed the police and told them what had happened. Because I was able to give a good description of the man—he had an ugly scar right across his forehead—the police captured him a short time later outside another house. He still had my ring in his pocket and his car was filled with stolen property. The police said the man had been responsible for more than thirty robberies in my area.

"The police officer who came to my house told me never to rely on uniforms as a means of identifying meter readers or other service company employees. City and state employees have their names, pictures and agency names clearly embossed or laminated on an I.D. card. If I had asked to see proper identification—not a business card or company literature—this crime might have not taken place.

"Also, the officer warned me to keep my screen door locked at all times because that would afford me an extra bit of protection when I open the front door. Talking to someone through the screen door is better than letting them get a foot in your door.

"I know I was lucky—I could have been killed on the spot. I'll never be so foolish again. Anyone who comes to my door from now on will have to show me some identification, or I just won't let them in. It's too bad things have to be that way," Emily sighed.

"I was lucky that time. I'm not about to push my luck again."

"Hello, Ma'am, how are you today?" the man said to Carolyn, adjusting his baseball cap and smoothing the blue work shirt that had "PAUL" stitched neatly in red across the pocket.

"I have a package here for Mr. Stern. Is he home to sign for it?"

Carolyn told him that her husband was away, and he asked if she would sign for it. "I just want to drop off the package and finish my deliveries early so I can head for the beach. This heat wave is killing me," he said, wiping some perspiration from his forehead.

He handed her the package and a pen.

"The pen's out of ink? Sorry about that. I don't seem to have another one handy," he said, sounding genuinely sorry.

"Do you have one? Great! And while you're at it, could I please have a cold glass of water. I'll just come inside for a minute to get out of the heat, okay?"

"Paul" told Carolyn he would wait in the hall, but after she let him inside, she heard him lock the front door as she walked toward the kitchen.

"Can you be more specific about the time?" Roberta asked the plumber whose name she had gotten from the telephone book.

"I'm not talking about a leaky faucet, Mr. Richardson. My toilet is backing up into my bathtub," she patiently explained once again to him over the phone.

"The best time to have one of your men come up here is today. Oh, that's impossible?

"Which nights will I be available? Well, let me see. Tuesday and Thursday nights I'm at my exercise class until 9 o'clock. Then we usually go for a bite to eat afterwards. Wednesday night I have a date after work so I won't be home until eleven.

"You'll send one of your men up as soon as possible? Thanks, Mr. Richardson. I appreciate it."

When Roberta's apartment was cleaned out that Thursday night, she learned an important lesson.

"The first time he came to my door he asked for directions to Chasen Road," Arlene began. "I told him I wasn't familiar with that road and closed the door.

"Several days later he rang my bell again and asked if he could use my telephone. He said he'd run out of gas and wanted to call his brother to come get him.

"I said if he gave me his brother's telephone number, I'd make the call for him. He said he didn't want to give me his brother's number because it was unpublished and his brother would kill him if he gave it out to anyone—especially a stranger.

"So I said, 'Okay, you can use the phone in the kitchen,' and he followed me there.

"I was getting a funny feeling about him—I felt uncomfortable. But I told myself I was just being paranoid.

"As quickly as he dialed he hung up, saying that there was no answer at his brother's house. He asked if he could use my bathroom and I said sure—anything to get him out of my house.

"Well, he took a real long time in there and when I went to see what the problem was, he was gone. I went to my bedroom and found that all my drawers had been emptied on the floor, my wallet was gone, as well as my emerald ring and pearl necklace.

"I know I never should have allowed a stranger into the house, but he looked like such a nice guy—neatly dressed, cleanly shaven—and he *had* come to my door earlier in the week.

"I never thought this kind of thing would happen to me. Being robbed was bad enough, but having to tell my husband—that was the worst." Arlene shuddered as she remembered the look on Dick's face when she told him of the day's events.

"He's always been after me to keep the door locked and the alarm turned on even when I'm in the house, and never, *never* to allow anyone I don't know into the house.

"I'd chide him for having such a suspicious nature, then tell myself I could do whatever I please. This was a hard way to learn a lesson."

SCREENING PEOPLE AT YOUR DOOR

Whether someone comes to deliver a package, steam your carpets, read a meter, sell you a vacuum, use your phone, or solicit for a charity, think carefully before you open your door to them. You are under no obligation to admit a delivery, sales or service person into your home.

Remember, you are the one who determines who crosses your threshold. Don't give con artists the chance to take advantage of you. The consequences could be devastating.

Alias James Rockford. Ask for identification and never settle for just a business card. Anyone can print up a batch of cards that say whatever they want on them.

Remember how TV private eye Jim Rockford would hand someone a business card he'd made up to suit his purposes when he carried out an investigation? Keep that in mind if someone uses a business card for identification. Take it, tell him you'll be right back and *close* the door. Go to the phone and ask the operator for the telephone number of the company whose name is printed on the business card. If there is no listing for the business, someone is trying to con you.

Don't go back to the door to demand an explanation of why there's no listing for the company this person supposedly represents. Instead, call the police and tell them what has happened. Hopefully, they will stop this person from taking advantage of others in the neighborhood.

Get the picture. For city and state employees, ask to see their photo identification card or badge. In the case of a plainclothes officer, a mere badge is not sufficient. Remember, anyone can buy a badge at a novelty shop or toy store. Instead, ask for a picture I.D.

Leave it outside. If an unexpected deliveryman comes to your door, and you are home alone, ask him to leave the package outside your door. If a signature is required, ask him to slide the slip under your door, then sign for the package and slide the slip back under the door. You can get the package after you're sure the deliveryman has left. (Here's where your wide-angle peephole comes in handy.)

Keep your schedule private. When you schedule an appointment for maintenance work, repairs, furniture delivery, rug installation, etc., don't disclose your personal schedule. By revealing the days and times when you'll be away, you leave yourself open to burglary. Unscrupulous people sell this information to thieves for a percentage of the loot. Instead, ask the company for *their* best time to do the work. Or say, "Monday and Wednesday mornings are best for me."

Phony emergencies. Criminals may try to gain entry to your home by faking an emergency. They'll tell you there's been an automobile accident, someone had a heart attack, their car broke down, or their wife is in the car in labor. They'll say anything to get inside your home. Then they'll ask to use your phone. As soon as you let them in, you've been had.

If an emergency phone call is necessary, offer to make it for them. Keep them outside while you make the call. If they tell you "never mind" when you offer to make the call or are gone when you return to the door, make a call to the police.

DATING SERVICES AND PERSONAL ADS

The same woman who would never allow a stranger into her home, pick up a hitchhiker, or give out her address or phone number to a stranger on the street, wouldn't hesitate to provide her personal life history—and pay a fee for the privilege—to a dating service. The person taking the information is dedicated to gathering as much personal information about her as he or she can in an attempt to find her a suitable date or two.

There are more than 72 million single people in this country, some of whom pay from several hundred dollars to more than $5,000 to be introduced to a selection of eligible dates, life mates, or even one-night stands.

If you've ever considered using a dating service, there are some things you need to know:

- Some services are completely fraudulent and are in the business of just taking your money and providing no service at all. By the time you catch on to the scam, they've disconnected their phones and moved their operation to another town, under another name.

- Some con artists use a dating agency as a "front" for a more lucrative business: burglary. By collecting the right kinds of information, under the guise of finding Mr. Right for you, they are able to learn when you're likely to be away from home and whether or not you have anything worth stealing.

Matchmaking is far from a perfect science, and the dating services field is virtually unregulated. As a result, there is great inconsistency in what agencies produce for their clients.

The safest way to find a reputable matchmaker or dating service is to seek recommendations from others who have had experience in this area. Once you've found an agency that sounds like it suits your style, call or drop by to ask a few important questions:

- How long has the company been in business?
- Is it registered with the local Chamber of Commerce and Better Business Bureau? (You can also check with small claims court. They will tell you if the agency has ever been sued.)
- How many members do they have in your age group and in your geographical area?
- Can they provide names of a few of their members who would be willing to recommend them?
- Who will come in contact with your personal file? Is it kept in a secured area?
- Exactly what they do they promise to do and when?
- What are their fees?

If these questions aren't answered to your satisfaction, look for another service.

Now a brief word about placing or answering personal ads. *Don't!* Unless, of course, you don't mind playing Russian Roulette with your life.

Think like a criminal. Wouldn't this be a great way to find a victim, without even having to leave home? Anyone who places or responds to a personal ad may have objectives other than meeting the perfect woman. Robbery and rape are two possibilities.

This method of meeting a man is fraught with too many unknowns to be safe. The possible dangers surely outweigh the risks.

Chapter 10

❖❖❖❖❖❖

Troublemakers
on the Phone

It is estimated by the Washington, D.C. based Alliance Against Fraud in Telemarketing that consumers lose about $10 billion a year to crooked operators of telephone scams.

These scams range from offering phony magazine subscriptions to selling worthless stocks. The proliferation of such rip-offs feeds on the willingness of the American consumer to purchase products over the phone.

BOGUS INVESTMENT SOLICITATIONS

P.T. Barnum once said, "There's a sucker born every minute." Con artists who operate on this premise make "chance-of-a-lifetime" offers to unsuspecting prospects every day. Usually, people who are in no financial position to sustain a loss are most likely to be taken in by these offers, but people who are quite wealthy have also been bilked.

In one scam, hundreds of consumers spent $5,000 each for 100 tons of unprocessed dirt, which was supposed to yield each of them 20 ounces of gold. In 1990, the so-called "dirt pile" gold scheme cost those investors $250 million.

If you are approached to make an investment by an individual or company that is unknown to you, you need to do some checking before you make a decision. You can obtain information on any stockbroker, registered representative, securities dealer or investment advisor by calling the National Association of Securities Dealers at 1-800-289-9999 to obtain information over the phone or to receive an Information Request Form before investing. This information is free to the individual consumer.

Follow these guidelines if you are approached to make any investment:

- If a "bargain" involves a substantial investment, take your time and consult your lawyer or accountant.
- Be especially cautious when you hear the word "guaranteed" used to describe investments. There is no such thing.
- Don't give cash to strangers or make checks out to an individual. And use a form of payment that allows you to cancel or stop payment.
- If you're unsure of a purchase, take the time to check it out through the Better Business Bureau or your state's attorney general's office.
- Don't be intimidated by high-pressure salesmen or tempted by a too-good-to-be-true offer. If it sounds too good to be true, it probably is.

CHARITY SCAMS

Turn on the radio, thumb through the newspaper, listen to the news on television. If a con artist needs some extra cash, all he has to do is pick up on a story or news item that's being focused on in the media and start his (or her) own charitable organization. How can you be sure you are dealing with a reputable organization and not just funding some scoundrel with a negative cash flow problem?

- Don't be pressured to make an immediate decision. The problems a charitable organization is trying to relieve won't be solved instantly with your donation.
- Give only to charities of your choice. Don't let high-pressure tactics make you feel guilty. If your choice is not to donate, simply say "No, thank you," and hang up the phone.
- Check them out. If you're not sure about an organization, check with the Better Business Bureau in your area, the state attorney general's office, or the Council of Better Business Bureaus.

- Never pay in cash. Pay only by check or money order made out to the charity's name—not to an individual.
- Never give out your credit card number over the phone to anyone who solicits you. Ask to have a pledge card sent to you. Only if you initiate a call to a known organization is it OK to give out your credit card information.
- Don't hesitate to ask for written materials that describe a charity's programs and finances before you donate. If the organization is reluctant to send this information to you, it's probably not a reputable group.
- If you receive unsolicited items such as address labels, greeting cards or calendars, you are under no obligation to return them or to donate money to the organization that sent them to you. It's against the law to demand payment for unordered items.
- Watch out for sweepstakes. Many organizations use them as a way of bringing attention to their cause. If you decide to participate in a sweepstakes, you do not have to make a donation. Before participating, be sure to read the sweepstakes rules carefully. Donors and non-donors should have an equal chance of winning.
- Be wary of telephone sales. Some groups sell household products such as garbage bags and light bulbs to raise money. This can be a legitimate fund-raising tool. But if you don't know the organization, get more information before placing an order.

If you want to do more research, The Council of Better Business Bureaus keeps tabs on organizations that solicit funds nationally or that claim to represent national or international causes. It has several publications designed to help make better decisions about donating.

Give But Give Wisely is a bimonthly list of charities that have generated the greatest number of inquiries to the C.B.B.B. It tells whether the charity meets the organization's standards for charitable solicitations. Copies are available for $2 sent with a stamped, self-addressed envelope.

Annual Charity Index includes brief program and financial summaries on more than 200 charities. Copies are available for $10.95.

PAS Reports are summaries of particular charities by the Philanthropic

Advisory Service. Inquiries are limited to three per person and are free. Include a stamped self-addressed envelope.

To order any of these publications, send a check or money order, if applicable, payable to the C.B.B.B. Foundation and mail it to:

Philanthropic Advisory Service
Council of Better Business Bureaus
Dept. 023
Washington, D.C. 20042-0023
(703) 276-0100

CREDIT CARD OFFERS

Phony promotions for major credit cards claim they will help you qualify for a low-interest credit card in exchange for a "processing fee," which can range from $70 to $200, charged to your current card.

The fee brings nothing more than a list of banks that charge low interest rates on their credit cards. This same list can be obtained free of charge or for a few dollars from consumer groups such as:

BankCard Holders of America
560 Herndon Parkway, Suite 120
Herndon, VA 22070
(703) 481-1110

INFORMATION THIEVES

Telemarketing fraud will continue to thrive as long as there's an unlimited supply of unsuspecting victims. Each time your phone rings and you are greeted by someone who is unknown to you, you need to question the validity of your caller's message.

"The caller said his name was Rob and that he was phoning to tell me I had won a trip for two to Hawaii," Claire said.

"I couldn't believe it. I'd never won anything in my life and here I was, going to Hawaii!

"'Rob caught the excitement in my voice, I'm sure, and started to tell me how beautiful this trip was going to be for my husband and me.

"He said he needed to ask me a few very simple questions and if I answered them, my tickets would be delivered in two days.

"Well, ask on, I said. And he did. He asked which credit cards I had. I told him. He said he needed to verify their numbers and asked me to give them to him. So I did—all of them.

"At the end of the week when I still hadn't received my tickets, I called the number he had given me and found that it was 'not a working number.'

"My charge cards, however, were 'working.' I was shocked to see my charge bills at the end of the month—each had over $2,000 in merchandise charged to my cards.

"I'm still trying to get these charges erased from my accounts. All I'd really won was a painful lesson about being naive."

Barbara and Ted were just sitting down to dinner when the phone rang.

"How are you this evening? My name is Phil and I'm with TV Surveys of America."

"Look, Phil, we're having dinner right now and..."

"No problem. This will really take only a minute of your time. I'm sure you are as fed up as most Americans are with the sex and violence that's being shown on the television these days. Am I right?"

"Yes, but...."

"That's why your participation in this survey is important. If you care about the quality of programming, then you'll help us out." Phil knew how to push the right buttons.

"Now, how many television sets do you have?"

"Three—one in the den, one in the kitchen, and one in the bedroom," Barbara replied, throwing Ted an exasperated look.

"Good. Now, how many people are home with you and when do all of you do most of your TV viewing?"

"Well, it's just my husband and me now. The kids are grown and on their own. I watch the talk shows every morning—my husband leaves for work before seven so he's never around to watch them with me. During the day, sometimes I might watch one of the soaps but never on Fridays because that's my day at the hairdresser.

"At night, Ted and I are usually in separate rooms because we don't like to watch the same programs."

"Well, thank you for your time," Phil said. Now, if you could give me your name and address, I'll send you out a gift certificate for a restaurant in your area to show our appreciation for your participation in our survey."

Barbara's number had been dialed at random by someone who was looking for a victim. She had just given out all the information any burglar would need if he wanted to rob a house (and one with three TV sets, at that) when nobody was at home.

SCREENING TELEPHONE INTRUDERS

Here are two ways you can deal with telemarketers, survey takers, donation seekers and potential telephone robbers if you choose not to put up with their intrusions:

- Stop the caller at the beginning of his spiel by saying, "Excuse me, is this a solicitation?" The caller may say he is only trying to give you information or obtain information that will somehow benefit you. Your response should be, "We do not accept telephone solicitations." Then hang up! Don't wait for any further reply—none is needed.

  If you feel uncomfortable being so abrupt, simply tell the caller that if he sends literature, you'll be glad to give the matter your consideration.

- Or try this: "This is an answering service. Would you like to leave your name and number?" This will almost always result in an immediate hang-up. If the caller persists in asking questions, you can repeat your original reply or simply hang up.

It's important to remember that these people are intruding into your privacy—usually at the most inconvenient times. In order to maintain control over the situation, get right to the point. Is this a solicitation? If it is, and you don't wish to be bothered, give one of the appropriate responses from above.

Many legitimate businesses do solicit by phone, but so do plenty of rob-em-blind prospectors armed with sucker lists. It's not easy to tell the good guys from the bad ones over the phone (or in person, for that matter). When in doubt, *hang up!*

STOPPING ANNOYING CALLS AND MAILINGS

If you wish to end those telemarketing calls or get rid of unwanted mail, the Direct Marketing Association asks you to put your request in writing and mail it to:

DMA
Telephone Preference Service   or
6 East 43rd St.
New York, NY 10017

DMA
Mail Preference Service
6 East 43rd St.
New York, NY 10017

DEALING WITH OBSCENE PHONE CALLS

Many of us will have to deal with an obscene phone call or some form of crank call at some time in our lives. An immediate and confident response will often deter a particular person from dialing your number again.

The typical obscene caller is a compulsive exhibitionist who chooses to shock verbally rather than visually (the flasher). These men are generally fearful of women and try to terrify them anonymously in order to prove themselves. The response of fear in their listeners excites them and pleases them sexually.

They choose their victims either by random dialing or by checking the newspaper. They look for photos and names of women who have been promoted within their company, engaged, married, recently divorced, given birth, etc., or they look for youngsters whose achievements (along with their name and photo) are noted in the local paper.

Then, they call Information for the telephone number of their chosen victim. To help avoid such calls in the first place, don't list a woman's first name in the telephone directory. A man's first name or initials are OK.

If you *do* find yourself at the other end of obscene or other crank calls, here's what you should (and shouldn't) do:

- Hang up immediately. Even just listening will egg the caller on.
- Do not engage in a conversation with him. Don't ask why he's doing this to you. If you need to be reminded, reread the previous paragraphs.
- Forget about reasoning with him. Remember, any response from you furthers his sexual pleasure.
- Blow a whistle into the phone if you have one handy.
- Tap the phone with your fingernail or pencil if the calls persist. Then say "Officer, he's on the phone again." (Do this only if you can sound convincing.)
- If annoying calls persist, keep an accurate time sheet

describing the nature of the calls, so you can report them to the police.

- Report annoying and abusive calls to the telephone company. They will advise you of what further steps you need to take before they put a tracer on your phone.
- Even one crank call threatening to harm you or your family warrants an immediate call to the police.
- An unusual number of hang ups or wrong numbers should also be reported to the police. They are one way criminals find out if someone is home.
- Make sure babysitters follow these rules and report any crank calls—no matter how innocuous they may seem.
- If all else fails, change your telephone number and have the new number unlisted.

THE ANSWERING MACHINE

Answering machines are both a blessing and a curse. They allow us the freedom to leave home or work, with the knowledge that we will not be missing important calls or social contacts. But they can also be used to provide clues to people who are looking for an empty home or office to rob.

If you have been getting an excessive number of hang-ups on your answering machine, you need to take a closer look at your recorded message. The hang-ups may not indicate anything serious—it just may be callers slamming down the phone in irritation at trumpet fanfares, sound effects, hit songs, or an excessively long message.

But there's a more serious problem with some of the recorded greetings people put on their machines—they might be inviting burglary: "I'm sorry I'm not home right now to take your call..." Or, what one women recorded on her machine as a message to her friends: "I'm on vacation in Bermuda. I'll be back in two weeks—on the twentieth..."

Messages such as these are nothing but a "go ahead, clean out my place while I'm gone" invitation to a prospective burglar. And, if he hears a message that tells how long you'll be away, he can take his time and empty your place at his leisure.

So, what *should* you say ? Keep it short and indefinite. Something like: "We can't come to the phone right now, but if you leave your name and number, we'll call you back just as soon as possible."

Don't mention your last name or phone number. People who know you already have this information, and you don't want to give it out to strangers who call.

Some callers may find an impersonal message irritating and feel that perhaps you are screening your calls and just don't want to speak with them. Don't let that concern you. It is far better to cause a little annoyance than it is to deal with the aftermath of a burglary.

Chapter 11

❖❖❖❖❖

Children Home Alone

Whether you plan to be away from home for only brief periods of time while you run errands, all day because of work, or the entire evening while you are out socially, you need to prepare your children to take care of themselves in your absence. Of course, the age at which you feel your children can be left alone will depend on their maturity and other individual circumstances.

On the negative side, youngsters who are left alone may be exposed to dangers that they must handle by themselves: physical injury, fire, robbery and assault. On the positive side, learning how to take care of themselves can help children become independent and will heighten their sense of self-esteem.

When you are convinced that you have done everything within your power to get them ready to care for themselves, you should start by leaving your children home alone for short periods of time at first and gradually build up to more extended periods.

SETTING THE HOUSE RULES

Once the decision has been made to leave your children home alone, carefully set up rules and helpful guidelines for them to follow when they are in charge of themselves.

The best protection you can give your children is to teach them how to:

- Recognize difficult situations.
- Avoid them if possible.
- React in the safest manner.

Schedule family meetings in which the rules and guidelines are discussed and understood by everyone involved. Post the rules in a prominent place such as on the refrigerator door or a family bulletin board. Make sure your children acquaint their friends with these rules and let them know that everyone is expected to abide by them when they are in your home. It is also a good idea to give each child a copy of the rules to post in his or her bedroom.

Here are some general rules you will want your children to follow. You may want to add to or delete from them as your particular situation warrants:

- Come directly home after school. Phone a parent (or other agreed upon adult) when you come in so someone knows you got home safely.
- Keep the doors locked at all times. Do not answer the door if someone rings the bell or knocks, unless you have been instructed otherwise. If you have been told you may answer the door, look out through a window or through the peephole to make sure you know the person.
- If you want to have friends in the house, you must first have your parents' approval.
- Obtain parents' permission to leave the house. Let them know where you will be.
- Limit phone calls to a few minutes so parents can call home when they need to.
- Do not give out personal information such as family name, number of siblings, or whereabouts of parents to callers.
- In an emergency, first call (list the police, fire department and poison control numbers), then call parents.

COPING WITH OUTSIDERS

Children can be made to feel at ease when they are left alone if they have been coached on how to deal with circumstances that are likely to arise. By teaching them clear-cut responses to these situations, the responsibility for making difficult decisions is lifted from their shoulders.

Two areas that children may have difficulty with are how to answer the door and how to handle phone calls. Because we teach our children to be polite to adults, children aren't sure how to balance good manners with personal safety concerns.

ANSWERING THE DOORBELL

Most of us know that opening a door to strangers is asking for trouble. However, what most parents don't realize is that opening the door part way (keeping the chain on) is almost as dangerous. It doesn't take much force to knock that chain off its wooden frame.

A stranger catching a child peeking out the window, or hearing her dragging a chair to the door to look out the peephole, may correctly suspect the child is home alone.

The best safety strategy is simply to teach your children to *never* let a stranger in. Any other action places them in danger and forces them to decide whether or not the stranger has a legitimate reason to be in the house. Kids want to be helpful and polite. Criminals know this and use it to their advantage.

If you need to have a delivery or repair made, schedule the appointment at a time when you will be home. If that's not possible, ask a neighbor or relative to be there in your place. If you're expecting a delivery, ask to have it left on your doorstep, in your lobby, or delivered to your neighbor. Don't put your children in an unsafe position.

HANDLING PHONE CALLS

It is important to teach your children how to deal with various types of phone calls. This helps lessen their fear and increases their confidence when they are home alone.

The best way for anyone to answer the phone is with a simple "hello." It is *not* a good idea to teach children to say, "This is the Smith's home, Michelle speaking."

It may sound polite, but do you really want a stranger to know your child's first name? He may call again, address the child by name, convince her he is a friend of the family, and elicit more personal information from her. The caller can also assume that a child who is careless about giving out information over the phone will be just as careless about locking doors or letting strangers into the home.

Here are a few situations your children may encounter:
- A caller says, "Guess who this is." Tell your children to

say, "I don't play guessing games on the phone." Then, hang up.

- Someone calls and says, "Hi, who's this?," "What number did I dial?," or "Where do you live?" Teach your children *not* to give out any personal information. Suggest that they respond with, "Who are you trying to reach?" If the questions persist, advise your children to hang up the phone.

- An obscene caller phones. Tell your children not to listen or talk, but to quickly hang up the phone. If there are more calls, they should unplug the phone or take it off the hook *after* they call you so you won't become alarmed should you try to phone home.

Help your children make up a convincing excuse to give when someone calls and asks if Mom or Dad is home. For instance, "Mom (or Dad) is

- in the shower/taking a bath.
- changing the baby.
- taking a nap and asked not to be awakened.

Find an excuse or two that your children are comfortable with. After practicing with them, ask a co-worker or trusted neighbor to phone home when you are not there to see how convincing your children sound. It appears simple, but without practice your children may get confused and give the wrong response.

PLAYING THE "WHAT IF...?" GAME

"What would you do if...?" games help children to consider *beforehand* how they would handle various safety situations.

For example, in the following situations, teach them that the best answer is, "I wouldn't open the door":

- A stranger rings the doorbell and tells your child that he is a relative who just arrived today for a surprise visit.

- A woman comes to the door with a floral arrangement and tells your child it is a surprise gift for mommy.

- A stranger tells your child he is there to repair the telephone line.

Teach your children that a "stranger" is anyone they do not know. Children often think a stranger is ill-kempt and dangerous looking. It doesn't matter how a person is dressed, what he says, or how friendly he seems to be. A stranger may have a legitimate reason for coming to your home, but your children cannot take a chance.

THE PARENT'S GUIDE TO BABYSITTERS

In a day where stories of abuses by babysitters and nannies abound we are aware that leaving our children in someone else's care makes them vulnerable.

You can provide the greatest measure of protection by being scrupulous in your selection of the babysitter or nanny and by assuring your children that you will take seriously what they tell you about the way they are treated.

Screen your babysitters. The best way to find competent and reliable sitters is through recommendations and character references from neighbors and friends. When you hire a babysitter, think of that person as a job applicant. When the job you're hiring for is as critical as this one, no amount of scrutiny is excessive.

Once you have checked out a prospective sitter, don't stop there. Make sure your children have the phone number of a neighbor or relative to call in case of an emergency.

Prepare your children for the babysitter. Talk about the rules you expect your youngsters to obey (safety rules, house rules, meal and bedtime rules). Also discuss which of the sitter's possible requests your children should not obey, such as being asked to do something that doesn't feel comfortable to them or being offered a special treat for not telling about something.

Explain to the sitter that your children don't keep secrets. They will tell you if something goes wrong and that they have permission to say "No" if they don't understand a request. If you carefully review the family rules, there will be less likelihood of a misunderstanding between the sitter and your children.

Make your rules clear to your sitter about having their friends over and the use of your phone.

Leave emergency numbers near the phone, as well as a phone number where you may be reached at any time. And don't hesitate to pay the sitter an unannounced visit or to call home while you're out to make sure everything is okay.

When Your Child Is a Babysitter

When *your* child is asked to babysit, remember that she (or he), too, is being put into a vulnerable situation. She is alone in a house she might not be too familiar with, and working for people she may not know well.

As a babysitter, your child has the responsibility for looking after the safety of young children as well as her own, and often she will be coming home late.

Have her meet her employers *before* she sits for them the first time. Assure her that if she feels uncomfortable with them, she need not take the job.

Have her work out her transportation to and from her job before she starts. (A ride from you is the safest.)

As a parent, know where, when and for how long (if possible) your child will be gone. Ask for the phone number where you can reach her, if need be.

Make sure she has the phone numbers of the police, the fire department, the neighbors, the children's doctor, and a number where she can reach the parents, in case of an emergency.

Tell her never to indicate to anyone who phones or rings the doorbell that she is the babysitter. Also, she should not allow the children to answer the phone or the door because they can be easily tricked into letting others know that their parents are not at home.

If she hears suspicious noises or someone tries to break into the house, she should take the children and get out of the house as fast as possible, provided there is an unobstructed exit. Otherwise, she should call the police immediately.

She should not confront an intruder nor leave the children unprotected.

Communication Is the Key

Parents and children need to speak with each other openly about safety and about ways of avoiding trouble. You cannot guarantee that your children will be completely safe, but you can reduce the risks by teaching them how to avoid potential dangers and by establishing good communications.

Teaching your children how to protect themselves cannot be accomplished in just one conversation. It must be an on-going process during which they learn by role-playing, repeating instructions, and playing the "What if...?" game.

If you make this teaching time an important family commitment, you'll have the peace of mind that comes with knowing you've done everything possible to keep your children safe and sound.

More Power . . .
At Work

Chapter 12

❖❖❖❖❖

Privacy and Personal Safety

From the very beginning which, in the case of a job, means when you apply for employment, there are certain rights to which you are entitled. One of the most critical of these is the right to privacy. Another is personal safety.

THE JOB APPLICATION

Some job applications are simple—they consist of just one page and ask for your name, address, telephone number, place of last employment and a few other particulars. Others are more extensive and ask for information regarding personal, medical, military, educational and employment history, and more.

Unless a question on the application violates Equal Employment Opportunity Commission (EEOC) legislation, employers have the right to ask for any information they want, provided they can prove it's useful as an occupational qualification. Employers may not, for example, ask for your marital status, whether you are pregnant, or if you have had an abortion. And polygraph tests have now been outlawed as pre-employment screening devices for almost all but government jobs.

Each time you fill out an employment application, you may be handing out a lot of personal information. If you're uncomfortable leaving personal information with a company that doesn't hire you, make every attempt to get your application back if you are not hired.

If you do get the job, legally that information no longer belongs to you, but to the company and, except in a few states, there is no restriction as to who can gain access to it. (Check your state's regulations.) You should be aware that often what you consider to be private, personal information may be available to various people in your company.

Because many companies process their own insurance claims, they have access to your complete medical history. Most insurance claim forms have a blanket waiver that authorizes the employer and insurance company to release or obtain any information necessary to determine payment of benefits. If you work in a small company, your boss may be the one to sign your claim form and read the insurance company's report on how the benefits were distributed.

It's a good idea to read through your personnel file from time to time (you may have to fight to gain access to it). See what notes and information have been put in there and if your privacy rights have been violated. If your company has a written personnel policy, it will contain a statement of your rights within the company.

If you believe that your right to privacy has been violated by your employer, you may wish to consider pressing charges against the company. Here are the steps you should take first:

- Study your company's personnel policy.
- Consider your employer's need to know the information gathered through the breach of privacy.
- Determine whether you have broken any company rules or policies.
- Discuss the situation with your employer.
- Document your communication with your employer and any significant events related to it.
- Find out whether others have been treated as you have—you may be able to join with them in a complaint.
- Get legal advice. Your local American Civil Liberties Union (ACLU) office can apprise you of national and state laws which apply to your situation.
- The ACLU can also recommend a lawyer experienced in employee rights litigation.

OFFICE SNOOPS

If you've been in the working world for a while, you may have come to think of your office as your private (and secure) domain. In fact, that may not be the case.

Having good rapport with your co-workers does not guard you completely against theft of personal possessions or freedom from intrusion.

Your best defense against work-related crimes is to be alert to situations which could cause problems and to use common sense in protecting your personal possessions and yourself.

> "I took a vacation day on Friday and when I returned on Monday, my office looked like it had been burgled," Cynthia fumed.
>
> "Files were strewn all over my desk, the cabinet drawers were ajar and my middle desk drawer, where I keep my personal notes, had been rifled. My boss said he had been looking for an important memo and had to go through everything to find it. He hadn't found what he was looking for, but I'm sure he did see a letter offering me a job at a competitor's company."

What if someone did need to find a report in your office while you were away? In pursuit of the missing file, would that person uncover personal items that you keep in your desk drawer that you would not want others to see—a letter from a headhunter, notes on a confidential project, love letters?

What are your rights of office privacy? Are the contents in your desk, file cabinet and closet your property or are they subject to search and seizure by curious co-workers?

Everything on company property, other than your personal effects (your clothing, purse, photos) belongs to the company. Office supplies, equipment, files, written material and, frequently, all the ideas you've conceived during business hours, are regarded, legally, as company property.

Common courtesy dictates that co-workers should not be rummaging through your drawers without your permission. But in nearly every office there are people who haven't heard of common courtesy. They'll "borrow" your scissors, your stapler, your tape dispenser and more—without a qualm.

And while they're searching for staples, they might as well see what else looks interesting. In their search for pens and pencils they can't resist opening and reading through the file stamped "CONFIDENTIAL" that you stashed way in the back of the bottom drawer, under stacks of other files, an umbrella and a pair of old sneakers.

Rifling uninvited through a co-worker's address book or card file is taboo. While looking for a particular telephone number is acceptable, browsing is not.

The methods people use to procure personal or confidential information are as varied and as challenging as those who attempt to use them. Some people make it a point to drop by your desk when they think you're working on something confidential, and some can even read upside down as they talk with you in your office. Of course, your computer screen can put confidential data within anyone's view.

If you are unexpectedly interrupted while you're working and you catch someone trying to peek at your computer screen or at confidential papers on your desk, ask the person to please leave the room, and promise to get back to them as soon as possible. If they don't leave, stuff your papers back in your drawer or into a file, or drape something over your computer screen until they get the message. If the intruder is offended, that's unfortunate. You did ask them politely to leave.

Stand your ground. If someone has a problem with your reaction, and tries to intimidate you into revealing classified information, remember, it's their problem. Don't make it yours.

If you are working on sensitive material, don't leave scribbled notes, open file folders or computer screens full of data unprotected in your office. If the information is personal and/or confidential, keep it that way by being particularly careful when leaving your desk.

> "I had been working for several weeks on a highly classified project," Marlena began.
>
> "I was amazed at the techniques some of my co-workers would use to persuade me to leak information. One woman tried to weasel some information out of me by implying that my boss was excluding me from access to important data. She told me I could prove her wrong by showing that I did, indeed, have access to privileged information."

KEEPING DATA PRIVATE

How can you protect your own privacy while providing access to business-related materials for those who actually should have it?

- Make it hard for the casual snooper to find confidential material. Give code names to sensitive subjects such as resumes, salary data, and performance appraisals and put them at the back of the bottom file drawer.

- Be sure to keep those who need to know informed about where important documents are kept.

- Don't try to protect all your files. Make sure those that aren't confidential are accessible, and let everyone who needs them know where to find them.

- Label the drawers "Work in Progress," "Client Files" and so forth. If the files can be found easily, there's little excuse for people to go through every drawer.

- If you feel these tactics won't stop people from snooping further, carefully seal sensitive material in a sturdy 9 x 12-inch envelope on which you have written your name or short message across the sealed section. Even the most curious will hesitate to open the envelope. Duplicating your handwriting on a fresh envelope is more of a challenge than most snoopers are up to.

- Don't tempt the sticky fingers of a thief. A good rule to remember is: If it's classified, sensitive, confidential or personal, on paper or disk, lock it securely in a desk drawer or cabinet and don't leave the key in the middle desk drawer. That defeats the whole purpose of security. No one but authorized personnel should have access to those files.

A Word to the Wise

While we're on the subject of revealing personal information to others, think carefully before you share personal information with a co-worker. Not only might that person pass your private conversation on to the wrong party, but your discussion could be overheard.

Two co-workers met for lunch in the company cafeteria. "Helen, swear to me that what I am about to tell you will go no further," Rosalie pleaded.

"Sure, sure. What's this all about anyway?" Helen put down her sandwich and gave her friend her undivided attention.

"Look, you know what I think about this job. My boss is completely incompetent—he can't make a decision to save his life. No one knows how to manage in my department."

"You're not going to change anything by complaining, Rosalie."

"I know. That's why I'm seriously thinking of leaving. I've had one job interview already and have two more scheduled next week—one at the largest ad agency in town."

"That's terrific. Tell me more about it!"

Later that day, Rosalie's boss called her into his office and repeated, almost verbatim, her lunchtime conversation with Helen. He terminated her immediately.

Rosalie ran back to her lunchmate. "How could you have done this to me? I told you everything I said was confidential."

"I don't know what you're talking about. I didn't tell anyone anything about our conversation," Helen said.

Obviously, someone at a nearby table in the lunchroom had repeated Rosalie's story to her boss. But Helen could just as easily have betrayed Rosalie's confidence.

A good rule to remember: If you don't want to say it to *everybody*, don't say it to *anybody*.

MUM'S THE WORD

Within all organizations, some topics are off-limits to outsiders. Employees are well advised to learn which kinds of information can be given out freely and which kinds must be withheld.

On a business level, disclosing information about salaries, contracts, pending litigation, merger proceedings, labor relations, credit reference information, and other closely guarded data is a no-no which can, in some instances, result in your termination.

On a personal level, confidential areas include co-workers' work schedules, absences, routes to and from work, and home phone numbers. You and your co-workers need to respect each other's privacy and should not give out personal information on the phone to anyone. Make it a part of your own office practice to keep personal information about co-workers to yourself, and expect the same from others.

Imagine that you are new to a job. The phone rings, you answer it, and a "husband" asks if his wife has come in yet. That probably sounds like the easiest question you've been asked all day, but don't be too quick to answer what may appear to be an innocent question.

Put the caller on hold and, if possible, go right to the person involved to ask if you should be giving out this information and, if so, to whom. If the person about whom the questions are being asked is unavailable, ask your supervisor about office policy regarding the release of this information.

If you still cannot get an answer (remember, you don't know for sure if you're really talking to the husband, boyfriend, father or someone else who has a legitimate reason for asking), tell the caller that you are new to the office. If he would like to leave a number where he can be reached, you will have the call returned.

Should someone persist in seeking information you are not free to disclose, you can tell him:

- I'm not at liberty to discuss this with anyone.
- I don't have all the information at this time.
- I'll discuss your request with Personnel and get back to you, if you'd like.

"Has Ms. Edwards arrived yet for her appointment?" may simply be the question of a caller trying to verify an appointment. On the other hand, it could be someone trying to gather information for any of a number of scurrilous purposes.

It's best that you familiarize yourself with office procedures regarding requests for personal information so you will be prepared to handle delicate situations when they arise.

> "A man who identified himself as an out-of-stater called the office and told Joanne, the receptionist, that he couldn't remember the name of the woman he was looking for, but gave her a vague description," Connie said.
>
> "He told Joanne that the person he was looking for was short and cute. That description fit several women in the office, but for some reason, she gave him my name."

During that brief conversation, Joanne told the caller Connie's full name and home address. When she asked if he would like to leave a message because Connie was away on vacation, the man said it wasn't that important and that he'd call again when she came back.

"It was a great vacation, but I was looking forward to getting back home. The minute I put the key in the lock, I knew something was wrong," Connie explained, twisting her engagement ring.

"I opened the door and walked into a completely empty apartment. There were no rugs, no furniture, no appliances—nothing. All my engagement gifts were gone. Even the phone had been taken. Except for a few clothes scattered on the floor, it looked as if no one lived there. I couldn't believe it," she said wiping the tears from her eyes.

Connie also remembered the startled look on a neighbor's face when she ran next door to call the police.

"My neighbor wanted to know why I was back so soon after moving and if my friends had forgotten to take something. He told me how nice they were and how lucky I was to have friends who would move me while I was on vacation. They even conned him into helping them load my things into the truck!"

Because more than a week had elapsed between the time she was burglarized and the time she returned home, the police told Connie that the chances of finding any of her belongings were slim. She might have prevented the burglary if she had left instructions about who should have been given her whereabouts, itinerary or phone number.

CRIME SCENES

Certain locations in every office cry out as sites for thievery or assault. These are the choicest ones:

The bottom drawer. Do you keep your purse in the lower drawer of your desk? Unless you are glued to your desk all day, or lock your door *every time* you leave your office, you are leaving yourself open to thievery, especially if your desk is near the front door, near a window, close to the ladies room, coat room, office supply cabinet or copy machine.

The best place to keep your purse and everything else of value is in a locked drawer or closet—and never in plain view.

The community closet. If you share a coatroom with fellow workers and/or clients, keep your coat pockets empty. If something is important to you and you don't want to lose it, it needs to be locked up. Never leave keys, identification, credit cards, check books or cash in your coat pockets if you use a shared closet. Even if everyone in your office is honest, visitors to the building may not be.

Isolated areas. Physical assaults and thefts in offices usually occur in isolated areas such as elevators, stairways and restrooms.

If the public has access to your restrooms, or if the restrooms are located in a remote area, be alert upon entering. If you sense danger, leave immediately and tell someone in authority.

Exercise caution when using the elevators—don't get into one if someone suspicious looking is the only passenger. And don't use the stairways, except in case of an emergency.

Working after Hours

Working late hours or coming in to work on the weekends can have its benefits. The quiet office affords you the opportunity to get more work done. However, it's also a good time to become a victim.

- Make sure you are familiar with your building's security system. If there is none, you must learn how to summon immediate help.
- If you must work late or on weekends, let someone know where you are and when you're expected to return home.
- If you feel uneasy about working after-hours, explain your feelings to your boss and try to work out a satisfactory solution to the problem. If that's not possible, find out who else is working overtime in your office. Try to coordinate your work schedules and/or exchange phone numbers in case of emergency.
- If you must sign in on a lobby ledger, use only a first initial with your last name.
- Turn on the lights in the main areas and in some of the other offices to make it look like there are people around.
- Have the phone numbers of building security right by your phone.
- If you encounter someone who looks or behaves in a suspicious manner, do not hesitate to call security.

WORKING ALONE

Whether you work alone in an office or in a retail establishment, you need to make special provisions for your safety. A little paranoia can't hurt in these instances:

- If you work in a high crime area, a good lock on the door and a security buzzer can keep trouble out and let your customers or clients in.
- Inform the security guard in your office building if you're in an office or a policemen on your beat if you're in a shop that you work alone and should be checked on periodically.
- Have a plan formulated ahead of time in case someone enters your premises looking for trouble. You should be prepared to hand over any cash or merchandise that is asked for to protect yourself from physical harm.
- Install a panic button that summons police or a security guard in case of emergency to provide a degree of protection.

WHEN YOU LEAVE THE OFFICE ON BUSINESS

Often, the very work you do can put you at risk of becoming a crime statistic. Certain jobs require that you leave the office. When you do, use common sense. If you must leave your office to meet with a client, or are leaving your office *with* a client, make sure *someone* knows where you are going, what it is you'll be doing, with whom, and when to expect you back.

You're probably thinking that everyone at your office is too busy with their own work to keep track of your schedule. But think of the consequences to your workmates and company if something were to happen to you while you were on office-related business. In addition to dealing with whatever injury or fright you suffered, your company would have to rewrite office policies and develop better safety plans for the employees. So why wait until someone gets into trouble to take precautionary steps? Insist that your company follows safety strategies *before* an incident takes place.

Put up a board with the names of everyone who will take part in the security system. Next to each name, the worker should enter where she is going and when she is expected to return each time she leaves the office on business. (An erasable board works well for this purpose.)

There could be columns for a telephone number and/or address where each worker can be reached. Then, if someone doesn't return within a reasonable amount of time, the police should be notified of where they were last seen.

Develop a "buddy" system. If you must meet a client in an unsafe area, have a co-worker go with you. Again, someone back at the office should have the destination and expected time of return to the office.

While on the road, it's a good idea to phone in every few hours. Apprise someone at the office of your whereabouts and next destination.

If you meet clients in your office, keep the door open if you can. If not, have a telephone signal set up with a co-worker in case of an emergency.

Meeting a client in his home or office puts you on his turf, putting him (temporarily) in charge. Assume control by assessing the rooms around you and the people present. Give the impression that you feel confident, even if you're feeling cautious. If you do go into a private home, note the location of the front door. In an emergency, it won't do to run into a closet.

BUSINESS PHONE SCAMS

Most people think that crank calls are only made to home phone numbers, but that's simply not true. Many scams are perpetrated on businesses, and they work pretty much like home phone scams.

Some telephone scams target businesses and solicit contributions to non-existent causes or organizations. A personable voice might also try selling ads for publications that don't exist or have very limited circulation.

There are callers who insist on payment of bills for services or products that were never ordered or delivered. Watch out for those who offer to make you a "good deal" on specialty merchandise that they ordered "by mistake" or say that they have "an overrun" and are selling at "cost."

Callers may try to give you the impression that they have sold you services or goods—like printer ribbons or copier supplies—in the past. You might feel embarrassed at not remembering their names and feel obliged to do business with them.

You can't afford to make spur-of-the-moment decisions. If an offer made by an unknown solicitor is good for a short time only, or if the caller refuses to give his name and number, you know you have a shady deal waiting to happen. Remember, whether you're at work or at home, when someone calls to offer you something that sounds too good to be true—it probably is!

Chapter 13

❖❖❖❖❖

Sexual Harassment

Women are taught that male attention is flattering. Just look at all the ads on TV and in magazines. But we are becoming aware that certain kinds of attention can be demeaning as well.

WHAT IS SEXUAL HARASSMENT?

Sexual harassment is not an expression of love; it is a demonstration of power. Men who sexually harass are not admirers, but bullies.

Sexual harassment can be difficult to prove. In that respect it's a lot like rape, because many of the incidents happen when there are no witnesses present.

In a report by U.S. Merit Systems Protection Board, it was revealed that seven out of ten women are sexually harassed at some time in their careers. It also showed that sexual harassment of government employees cost the government $189 million in one 2-year period, as a result of low morale, lost productivity, absenteeism and employee turnover.

Sexual harassment is not an issue of sexuality in the workplace. It *is* an issue of power politics in which unwanted verbal or physical sexual conduct is sometimes used to influence career mobility—a mobility which should be evaluated solely on the basis of merit.

Many of us have felt unnerved by sexually threatening behavior, although the expression of it may have varied—from an unwanted lingering look or a hand in the small of the back, to sexual innuendos that occur far too frequently despite assurances of "just kidding," to blatant requests for sexual favors, to even rape.

"I was suddenly assigned to the dreaded midnight shift in the computer center of the international law firm where I worked," Janice explained.

"My assignment was announced at the weekly meeting by my supervisor, the same man who had repeatedly asked me to sleep with him."

Laura, an assembly-line worker said, "I was let go and told that I would be rehired when work picked up. Three people who were hired after me weren't laid off. According to our union's "bumping" rights, they should have been laid off first. But *I* was the one who reported my supervisor for sexual harassment."

According to the Equal Employment Opportunities Commission (EEOC), the federal agency charged with enforcing Title VII of the Civil Rights Act:

> Unwanted sexual advances, requests for sexual favors and other verbal and physical conduct of a sexual nature constitute sexual harassment when:
>
> 1. Submission to such conduct is made a term or condition of an individual's employment.
> 2. Submission to or rejection of such conduct is used as the basis for employment decisions.
> 3. Such conduct unreasonably interferes with work performance, or creates an intimidating, hostile or offensive working environment.

Men, as well as women, can be victims of sexual harassment and women, as well as men, can be the harassers. The harasser does not even have to be of the opposite sex. Since sexual harassment is a form of sex discrimination, the crucial issue is whether the harasser treats a member or members of one sex differently from members of the other sex.

It's also possible for the victim to be someone other than the person at whom the unwelcome sexual conduct is directed. It may be someone who is affected by such conduct when it is directed toward a third person. For example, the sexual harassment of one female employee can create an intimidating, hostile or offensive working environment for another female (or male) co-worker.

A finding of unlawful sexual harassment does not necessarily depend on the victim's having suffered economic injury as a result of the harasser's conduct. For example, improper sexual advances which do not result in the loss of a promotion for the victim or the termination of the victim may still constitute sexual harassment if they unreasonably interfere with the victim's work or create a harmful or offensive work environment.

What Are a Boss's Responsibilities?

All employees should be allowed to work in an environment free from unsolicited and unwelcome sexual overtures. Employers who know that their employees are being subjected to any form of sexual harassment have a legal duty to rid the workplace of that harassment. There are several steps an employer can take to affect a change, including:

- Acknowledging to the victim(s) that a problem exists.
- Expressing strong disapproval to the harasser(s).
- Developing appropriate sanctions.
- Informing employees how to raise and pursue their Title VII right to be free from sexual harassment.
- Sensitizing all concerned.
- Developing preventive programs tailored to each individual circumstance.

How Far Is Too Far?

Workers of both sexes should know their rights. They should be able to recognize when they are being made to feel uncomfortable and when they are making someone else feel uncomfortable. That doesn't mean that office romance is totally dead, but it does mean that there are definite rules to the game.

How can you tell if you're being sexually harassed? Sexual harassment can manifest itself either physically, psychologically or both ways. It can include verbal innuendos and inappropriate gestures.

Physically, you may be the victim of pinching, grabbing, hugging, fondling, being brushed against or any other form of touching. Psychologically, it can involve everything from relentless proposals of physical intimacy, perhaps subtle at first, to overt requests for sexual favors.

Often, the implicit message from the harasser is that non-compliance will lead to reprisals. That means you can expect demotions, transfers, undesirable work assignments, unsatisfactory job evaluations, sabotaging of your work, denial of raises, benefits and promotions and, in the end, job dismissal and a poor work reference.

The harasser has given you a choice—give in to his sexual demands or suffer the consequences.

Unfortunately, as with most sex crimes, when a charge is made, it is frequently the victim's behavior that is scrutinized, more than the perpetrator's.

> "Eric began making sexually suggestive remarks to me the first week on the job," Kate began. "Also, he would walk into my office and if I happened to be at my desk, he'd come over, bend down and put his arm around my shoulder, trying to look down my blouse.
>
> "It made me feel very uncomfortable, but I would tell myself I was just being foolish—that he was only being friendly. I saw him do it to other women and no one complained. I'm a single parent with two school-age kids. I was grateful to get this job, and I didn't want to jeopardize it in any way.
>
> "When I finally asked him not to touch me, and told him that it made me feel uncomfortable, he laughed and said, 'You're divorced, right? It figures. What you need is a man in your life to make you feel like a woman again.' And I thought these macho menaces had gone the way of polyester leisure suits!
>
> "In the span of a few months, he repeatedly propositioned me and continued to touch me, despite my protests. They just seemed to egg him on.
>
> "When I complained to my supervisor, Eric denied the allegations and said I had made sexually suggestive comments to him. Can you believe that?
>
> "My supervisor called a meeting with Eric and other women in the department, but "forgot" to tell me about it. With Eric and his supervisor in the room, the women were supportive of Eric.
>
> "My company made no further investigation, nor did it give me the opportunity to present my case to my co-workers or to confront Eric.
>
> "During this same period, I was denied a promotion to another department, supposedly because I wasn't qualified. They tried twice to transfer me to another facility—out of sight, out of mind—but I refused. So, they fired me a few weeks later. They hadn't told me the transfer was mandatory."

Kate filed a civil lawsuit and won a settlement of nearly $300,000 from her former employer for back pay and compensatory and punitive damages.

"It was a long time coming," Kate said with a sigh. "I just hope that hearing about my lawsuit deters guys like Eric from trying the same moves on other women."

SEXUAL HARASSMENT SYNDROME

Having to fend off sexual harassment every working day causes tension, anxiety, frustration and anger. Because it takes time and energy to deal with a harasser, job performance suffers. The anger is often internalized as a deep sense of guilt.

Physical ailments caused by the anxiety and frustration of being a victim of sexual harassment may include headaches, nausea, insomnia and other medical illnesses.

When you are involved with sexual harassment, the most important thing to remember is to protect yourself, and to refuse to feel guilty or responsible in any way for your problems. You are a victim and are in no way to blame for being the target of this *illegal* behavior.

Sexual harassment in the workplace is finally being acknowledged, and it is no longer just a "woman's" problem. Employers are clamping down on illegal behavior because they fear expensive litigation and a decrease in employee productivity. Ignoring the existence of sexual harassment can be a costly mistake.

STICKING TO BUSINESS

Business lunches and working dinners are often part of conducting business. They provide a chance, in a relaxed environment, to learn more about the critical aspects of your job, a way for your boss and co-workers to learn how serious you are about your work, or an opportunity to persuade a potential client to sign on the dotted line.

Much of the confusion about business etiquette is centered around the new roles men and women play in the business world. And the distinction between business and pleasure can easily become blurred unless you take great care to keep them separate.

Think twice before stopping for a drink with a male business associate after working hours. Men who have always behaved with perfect decorum in the workplace may become aggressive after a few drinks.

Only you can decide which lunches and dinners are legitimately for business only and which may lead to sexual harassment. Try to assess beforehand the underlying purpose of the meeting. Is it to establish or strengthen future business considerations, to discuss office policy, to learn what's happening in other departments that could affect your work, or is it just an excuse for an intimate get-together?

If you suspect that the objective is pleasure and you're only interested in business, don't accept the invitation. However, if you feel that you might have something substantial to lose by refusing to go, and you don't want to risk it, ask a co-worker or two to join you at the meeting. Or make it known that you have a male protector—husband or boyfriend (real or imagined) to serve as a deterrent to sexual overtures. If the man is married, talk about his family (and yours), making reference to them at every opportunity.

Don't ask for special favors. Avoid becoming indebted to a potential sexual harasser; he may try to collect what he believes is coming to him.

Out of Town Meetings

When you are out of town at a seminar or convention, remember that such occasions are business, not social situations. (See Tall, Dark and Deadly in Chapter 17)

When you go out for the evening, think of it as an extension of the work day. Plan to meet at a restaurant or in the hotel lobby. Avoid revealing your room number, and ask the hotel not to give it to anyone.

The potential sexual harasser may ask you pointed sexual questions. Steer conversation back to your career and work. Avoid behaviors that suggest you view the situation as a social encounter. Women who take their careers seriously should politely refuse to turn a business situation into a social one.

End the evening in a public place such as the lobby or restaurant. If a man offers to escort you to your room, you can always say, "Thanks, but that won't be necessary. I've really had an enjoyable evening." Then leave.

Confronting Sexual Harassment

If a sexual innuendo disturbs you, never ignore it. Confront the harasser immediately with your feelings. (Of course, this is easier said than done; confrontations are rarely easy.) However, choosing to ignore the problem, making excuses for the behavior, or feeling that there's something wrong with you for getting upset, will only encourage the offender to continue the harassment.

If someone persists in bothering you, say loudly, "I'm not interested in a social relationship, and I would appreciate it if you would stop harassing me!" This should, of course, embarrass him, especially if there are a lot of people around, but so what? Remember, it's his problem. Don't make it yours.

Talk with your co-workers. If other women have been harassed by the same person, ask them to join you in a complaint to your supervisor.

WHEN ALL ELSE FAILS

If you've confronted your harasser directly with no result and have spoken to your supervisor and still feel that you are not being heard, take yourself directly to the Equal Employment Opportunities Commission (EEOC). (Check your phone book under U.S. Government Offices for your local office.) Even though sexual harassment is a federal offense, laws in this area vary from state to state. Check with your own state agency for specifics, to be sure you follow the proper procedure for filing a complaint!

At an EEOC or a state or city human rights agency, file a discrimination complaint. You cannot file a lawsuit without going through this step. Complaints to the EEOC must be filed within a given number of days (usually 180) from the date when you were sexually harassed.

At the EEOC, a counselor will help you file a claim to make sure it fits the technical requirements of Title VII and the agency. A notice will then be sent to your employer (usually within ten days of filing) stating that a claim has been made and explaining the illegality of any retaliatory measures taken against you for making a claim.

The EEOC will investigate the claim and attempt to mediate a solution, working directly with the complainant and her employer. Generally, if a claim filed with the EEOC is not settled to your satisfaction within 180 days (check the exact number with your state), you may request a right-to-sue letter and you can then file suit under Title VII in the federal courts.

You have 90 or so days (again, check your state) to file this lawsuit, and it's crucial to have a lawyer ready to argue your case.

Litigation can be frustrating, time-consuming and expensive. On the other hand, a lawsuit can cost the employer time, money, bad publicity, embarrassment and may end in a negative judgment for him.

Legal pressures aside, more and more employers are realizing that harassment is not just a personal problem between two employees, it can affect the entire company. It costs companies money to ignore sexual harassment.

If you believe you have been the victim of sexual harassment, follow these simple guidelines:

- Don't ignore the harassment or feel guilty.
- Assess your options.
- Keep a log or diary of offenses in a secure place (not your desk).
- Write a letter to your harasser setting down your complaints, and in the last paragraph state how you want his behavior to change. Keep a copy for your personal files.
- Put your formal complaint in writing; and follow it through as far up the company hierarchy as you need to in order to affect a change.
- If all else fails, seek outside help from the EEOC in your state.

It takes courage to challenge people on what is and isn't acceptable behavior. When women come forward consistently to complain about offensive behavior, the message will eventually get across that sexual harassment will not be tolerated.

Chapter 14

❖❖❖❖❖

Powerful Communication

The single most important tool in business is communication. And there are two major ways in which we communicate—with words and with body language.

SEE WHAT I'M SAYING

What we say with our bodies—our facial expressions, our hands, the way we walk—often speaks louder and clearer than the words and sentences we choose. And it's harder to lie with body language than with speech.

If it only takes a criminal a few seconds to size you up as a victim—to decide whether he "likes" you enough to make your life miserable—think about the field day that the person who's "gunning" for you in your office can have when he can size you up at his leisure.

But even though body language is a critical means of communication, many people don't give it the attention it deserves or use it as effectively as they could. To project a more positive image, nail biters and hair-twisters should learn how to control their nervous mannerisms. People with poor posture and an apologetic walk should learn to stand up straight and walk with more confidence.

Some women set themselves up to be victims without realizing it. Does anybody wish to be ignored, laughed at, patronized, or worse? Of course not. So why are some women treated like that? Simple. Their body language screams, "Wimpy, wimpy, wimpy!"

In business, body language is simply another weapon in your self-defense arsenal, and an extremely effective one at that. Having an understanding of body language will make it easier for you to send effective messages to those with whom you come in contact. It will also help you understand other people and even to tune into messages they may not mean for you to get.

If someone says to you that he's not angry, but does it with a red face, bulging neck veins and a clenched jaw, can you believe him? Read his body language.

If you've just made a dynamic sales presentation and the prospective buyer says, "That's very interesting," all the while drumming his fingers and looking around the room, should you rush to get out the order book?

People are frequently judged more by their words than by their body language. But when one contradicts the other, the body language usually tells the real story.

The effectiveness of your communications will help determine your success in business life. Since body language works either for you or against you, it makes good sense to make it an asset.

Testing Your IQ (Image Quotient)

The way you carry yourself—the message you subconsciously transmit through nonverbal behavior—is a good indication of whether you're perceived as a wimp or a winner. Does your body language project the desired image? Take this quick quiz and find out. (Answer yes or no.)

1. Do you have poor or tense posture?
2. Do you keep your arms folded across your chest when sitting in a meeting or in the boss's office?
3. Do you avoid making eye contact with people?
4. Do you walk unilaterally, moving the same arm and leg forward and back at the same time?

How did you score? Be honest. Did you answer "no" to every question? If you did, you're definitely a winner and may move on.

If you answered "yes" to one or more questions, stick around. We've got work to do.

The Gender Gap

Through socialization, men and women are taught certain behaviors in accordance with their respective genders. Women are taught socially subordinate behaviors and are rewarded for them. Women have been trained to be constantly pleasing to others by keeping quiet, by smiling, and by agreeing with others' values and opinions.

This deferential behavior often causes us to stumble on the career ladder rather than climb it. Here's the double standard: When a woman is perceived as being strong-minded, she may lose respect; colleagues, bosses and sometimes friends say she is too aggressive.

Men have learned to expect subordinate behavior from women. They are often shocked, insulted or even outraged when women fail to behave as the stereotyped sex roles dictate.

So, how do you combat the effects of years of negative stereotyping? Too meek, you're a wimp; too assertive, you're a bitch. You need to cultivate and use a different kind of authority than men. Powerful and effective communication is created by actions, not by gender. And, walking a fine line, you have to combine several techniques in a subtle way.

FIRST IMPRESSIONS

When you walk into someone's office, that person takes only a few seconds to evaluate your entrance. The way you carry yourself can put them in a receptive frame of mind, so that they are anxious to hear to what you have to say, or it can convince them to get rid of you as soon as possible.

One trick to making a successful entrance, someone once said, is to pretend you are walking towards a person who is about to hand you a prestigious award. Imagine how receiving such an award would make you feel. As you confidently walk towards the person, your head is held high, your shoulders are back and relaxed, and you dazzle them with a warm smile that says, "I'm genuinely pleased to be here." If you follow that with direct eye contact and a firm handshake, you are bound to get a positive reaction.

The confident woman has a strong stride, a friendly smile, good posture and a genuine sense of energy. When she asks for respect visually, she usually gets it.

YOUR HANDSHAKE

To further solidify your presence, a good, firm handshake is a must.

Have you ever held a dead fish in your hands? You know how it just lays there, clammy to the touch. Think about *your* handshake. Could it be described this way? Or are you the "just the first four fingers, please," kind of woman?

There are two reasons why women shake limply or with their fingertips. Some women are not comfortable shaking hands at all, but do it because they've been told it's the thing to do; other women have been victims of "The Bone Crusher." They prefer to test the waters first before diving in completely.

Your handshake is a form of nonverbal communication and says a great deal about you. If you are really uncomfortable shaking hands, then don't offer your hand first. (But realize that this can be a mistake, especially if you want to make people like you, feel comfortable with you and, most importantly in this case, want to do business with you.)

However, when the decision has been made for you (an extended hand is in front of you waiting to be acknowledged), shake it with confidence— which includes a firm grasp and a direct look into the person's eyes.

For some men, a bone-crushing handshake may be a way of sending a message of power and control. Often these men do not have as much power and control as they would like others to think.

Other men have overzealous handshakes because they're gregarious people, comfortable with themselves and their surroundings, intending no harm to anyone. With this kind of fellow, you may just need to grin and bear the pain, or simply say, "Wow, you really have a strong grip," and hope that he remembers to be more gentle the next time you meet. Share some humor with him about his grasp or just let it go.

THE EYES HAVE IT

In business and social situations, eye contact is critical. Without it, we get only fragments of information. Whether you're speaking to an audience of one or 101, nothing is more crucial in communication than direct eye contact.

When you're speaking to a group of people, don't stare over their heads. Make eye contact with people in different sections of the room. Consciously or not, we all form initial opinions of people based on how they communicate with their eyes. Maintaining eye contact also affords you the opportunity to gauge reactions to what you are saying.

If you are conducting a meeting, it's very easy to use eye contact to control who speaks and who doesn't. When you look at someone and nod or show interest, you are giving the speaker permission to talk. If several people are talking at the same time, the one who garners the most direct visual attention will end up holding the floor.

When you're speaking to one person, eye contact is a sign of both reassurance and power. Make eye contact as soon as the other person begins to talk. This shows you are paying attention and are interested in what that person is saying.

Non-assertive women will look a man in the eye only if he is speaking to her, but not when she is speaking to him—then she'll lower her eyes or look to the side. Confident, assertive women maintain eye contact when they speak—with everyone!

If someone refuses to maintain eye contact with you it can indicate that you are being ignored, and that who you are and what you are saying is not important to them. Or it may indicate that the person feels threatened by you. If you are saying or doing something that makes the other person uncomfortable, consider your attitude and try to put the person at ease.

YOUR SMILE

There is nothing wrong with smiling if it complements your spoken message or the message that someone is giving you. In fact, if you are reluctant to smile, you will be considered stiff and unfriendly. In some circumstances, a smile or sense of humor can be just what's needed to diffuse a tense situation. Don't underestimate the positive effects of appropriately placed warmth or humor.

But if you smile in a nervous or forced manner, or smile inappropriately for no reason at all, you send out confusing messages and undercut your words.

Smiling, while speaking seriously, says that you have an eagerness to please—that you want others to think you are nice even though what you may be saying is not. This eagerness to be liked can come across as weakness. Rather than smiling constantly, pay attention to your facial expressions and make sure they match what you're saying or hearing.

RELAX!

Bette, a graphic artist, dreaded the weekly sales meetings. It wasn't that she was never prepared; she was. But her interactions with her associates at times left her feeling frustrated.

> "I would present my work and I would be humored, interrupted, negated or ignored.
> "I began to feel invisible and inconsequential. I asked more

questions than my male associates and introduced more ideas, but all I got were minimal responses or silence when I finished speaking."

Past experience told Bette that no matter what she said in those weekly meetings, she would not receive a favorable response. She subconsciously set herself up to fail by thinking, "I don't know why I bother to express my ideas because they will only be ignored." She finally realized her language and verbal communications were at odds with each other. And nonverbal communications always win out—it's what you don't say that counts.

It's extremely important to examine non-verbal behaviors in your quest for success. Make a concerted effort to alter those non-verbal behaviors that signal helplessness.

- Relax! Restricted movement and tension is characteristic of lower status communicators.
- Open up. A closed posture, such as round and slumped shoulders, communicates vulnerability and lack of confidence. Tense posture is indicative of a submissive attitude, giving you a "guarded" look.
- Stand tall and move assertively and with confidence.
- Make it a practice to keep your hands below your neckline. If you twist your hair or fiddle with your earrings, you'll appear to be nervous or possibly even flirtatious.
- Be sure your movements say what you're thinking. For example, when you nod, you are agreeing with something. But nodding, like smiling, is not always appropriate, especially if you want to end a dialogue. Too much nodding encourages the speaker to continue. To have your say, stop nodding, and assume a neutral expression.

Changing these behaviors will put you more in control and will improve your communication skills. You'll stop sending out submissive signals, and decrease the likelihood that you will be viewed as a target for victimization.

On Location

The location where a meeting is held can actually help or hurt you. Note, for example, that few people have ever been fired in their own offices; that usually happens on someone else's turf.

Are you planning a meeting? Then by all means hold it in your own office. It gives you a definite advantage. It puts you in control. Others will be on *your* turf—even if they are your superiors in rank. They are aware they have entered your domain and will accord you certain rights and privileges.

Control the seating arrangements. When the meeting begins, be seated in the power position—behind your desk.

What can you do if you don't have an office? Try to arrange the meeting in a neutral place—a conference room, or outside the company in a restaurant or hotel meeting room. That way, no one can claim the space; it's nobody's property.

Be smart and position yourself in the most advantageous place within the seating arrangement—at the head of the table, if you are conducting the meeting, or right next to the person who is.

Do you really want to assume control? Then spread your papers, pens, notes, folders, and anything else you brought with you over as broad an area as possible.

If you anticipate problems from someone at the meeting, sit right next to that person rather than across from him or her. It's very difficult for someone to argue with you when you are in this non-confrontational position. By breaking down the physical distance, you are also breaking down some of the emotional distance.

If, on the other hand, you are anxious to debate your adversary, sit directly across from him or her.

As the meeting gets underway, try to read the body language of others in the room. Folded arms don't always mean someone is turned off or has tuned you out. It could be that the person is cold or finds it to be a particularly comfortable position.

But if the folded arms are accompanied by narrowed eyes, tense shoulders and a skeptical facial expression, or the person is constantly looking at his watch, it's obvious he isn't too pleased with you or what you're saying. If that's the case, be direct. Say, "I see you're checking your watch. Do you have another appointment?" Or, "Should we continue this discussion another time?"

VERBAL CUES

Now that you've gotten your body language under control, you should be free to concentrate on what you say and how you say it. And also consider how you are spoken to by others.

How are you addressed at work? Terms of address can indicate the level (high or low) at which a person is perceived. Look around your office. More than likely, the people who are addressed formally (Mr., Dr., Ms.) have more power than those who are addressed on a first name basis. (Of course, in a company where all the executives are on a first name basis with one another, if you are referred to as "Miss so and so," your status is likewise lowered.)

The status lies in how one is addressed in relationship to other co-workers. If you feel uncomfortable with the way you are addressed (either too formally or too informally), insist on being addressed as you wish. How others address you will set the stage for the way you are perceived.

Is your speech assertive or submissive? Submissive speakers are hesitant and self-disparaging. They often qualify their remarks with phrases such as: "This is probably a stupid question, but . . .", "I was just wondering" or "This may not be important—but . . ."

Practice speaking with authority. Never cover your mouth with your hand as you speak, indicating that you are embarrassed about what you are saying. Use declarative sentences. Be firm and assured in your delivery. For example, say, "I read the proposal and want to discuss several areas which I find ambiguous," rather than, "I was wondering if you thought that we might be able to get together to talk about the proposal."

Don't feel you must respond to the pause after a superior speaks. Silence is often used to embarrass or disorient low-status communicators who feel they must fill in lulls in the conversation. Do not feel you must "jump in" to fill the void.

Choose your words with care. Well crafted sentences tell the listener that you are bright, thoughtful and worth listening to. Don't be shy about using language that makes you sound intelligent and expressive. Once you get used to using the full range of your vocabulary, you'll wonder why you didn't make better use of your assets before. A lot of "ya know"s and "like I said"s won't command the kind of respect you seek.

Use your voice to advantage, to make yourself sound decisive.

- Turn on enough volume to be heard.
- Keep the pitch of your voice low.
- End sentences with a downward inflection.

Combining these techniques will earn you attention and respect.

THE PICTURE YOU PORTRAY

Be observant of your own non-verbal behaviors and that of others. Watch people around you. Evaluate how their movements and body language make them appear more vulnerable.

Then, evaluate your own strengths and weaknesses. By projecting yourself in a forthright manner, you have nothing to lose—and everything to gain.

Be determined to overcome any fear you might have. Walk and speak with confidence (yes, even when you don't feel it).

Positive, self-assured people energize others around them. Be genuinely enthusiastic and confident. Value yourself. Everyone likes to be associated with confidence and success.

The truth of the matter is, people react to you as they perceive you to be. Learn how to create positive perceptions of yourself to achieve personal and professional success.

More Power . . .
When Traveling

Chapter 15

❖❖❖❖❖

Preparing for Your Trip

Nothing should be allowed to spoil the wonderful vacation you have planned or the successful business trip you envision, but unless you take some precautions when traveling, it's possible that an unfortunate incident just may intervene.

The threat of theft or bodily harm exists when you travel, just as it does when you're at home, but you can increase the likelihood that you'll travel safely if you follow a few simple rules and exercise a reasonable amount of common sense.

PRE-VACATION CHECKLIST

Whether you're planning to be gone for a few days or a few months, you need to take the necessary steps to secure your home before you leave. Many homes are broken into and vandalized while the owners are out of town because it is clear to anybody who is watching that nobody is at home.

If you haven't already conducted a security survey of your home, it's essential that you do so before you leave for a vacation. In many communities the police will conduct this survey for you, advising you of the vulnerable points of entry to your home and the protective measures to make your home more secure. If you do the survey yourself, go through the "Home Security Checklist" in Chapter 6 and do whatever is necessary to secure your property and afford yourself peace of mind while you're away.

Take these additional precautions when you plan to be away for a prolonged period:

- Tell only those who absolutely need to know that you'll be away. The fewer people who know about your trip, the safer your home will be.
- Make sure your garage doors are secure; don't forget to lock any doors inside the garage too. If you plan on taking your car, cover the garage windows so burglars can't see the car is not there.
- Don't help the thief; keep all tools and ladders secured and out of sight.
- Arrange for a neighbor or trusted friend to keep an eye on your home, gather your mail and newspapers, share some of their trash with you on garbage day, mow the lawn or shovel the snow, and park one of their cars in your driveway. You want your house to have that "lived-in" look.
- Place several lights, and a radio or television on automatic timers.
- Don't keep all your curtains or shades tightly drawn unless this is the way they always are kept. Instead, close a few, leave others partly open.
- Trim all shrubbery which blocks windows or doorways as it provides a burglar with a hiding place.
- Unplug your phone or turn down the ringer so no one can hear it going unanswered.
- If you have an answering machine, don't change your message to, "Gone on vacation. See you in two weeks." And don't invite burglars in by posting that message on your front door!
- Take your spare house key and give it (along with your itinerary) to a trusted neighbor or relative. Ask that she periodically check your home to make sure everything is in order.
- Don't tempt the thief by packing your car the night before you leave. It's an open invitation to burglars and it telegraphs the fact that you'll be gone for awhile.

REQUESTING A ROOM

When making a room reservation, be sure to choose a reputable hotel located in a low crime area of town, then request a room following the guidelines below.

Unless you're a frequent guest at a particular hotel, you won't know where your room will be until you're actually in it. By that time, if you wish to change rooms, it may be too late. However, with a little up front planning, you can make your preferences known at the time you reserve your room to avoid potential problems later.

Ask for a room that is:

- Not on the first floor (where windows are easily reached and accessible to criminals).
- Not by the ice, soft drink or snack machines (where people may loiter without arousing suspicion).
- Not next to elevators, stairs or fire-escapes (where it's too easy for criminals to get to or from your room).
- Not located where you must walk through long, deserted corridors.

The best room to have would be on the second floor or higher, preferably in the middle of the corridor, and not too far from the elevator or staircase or other means of access and exit.

In better hotels, concierge floors are popular among the security conscious because they almost always have restricted access; a special key is needed for the elevator to stop on those floors.

Advise your hotel to hold your room if you will be arriving late so you won't be forced to find alternative lodging.

PLANNING AHEAD

Before departing, double-check to make sure you have packed those special items that cannot be easily replaced: medicines, eyeglasses or contact lenses, credit cards, and so forth.

If you have a homeowner's policy, check to see if it covers your luggage and/or its contents. If it doesn't, and you are taking expensive items with you (for example, jewelry, camera equipment or furs), you may wish to purchase a trip insurance policy, which is available at reasonable cost. And make an inventory of the valuable items you are bringing with you. Leave one copy at home in a safe place and bring the other with you.

If you'll be traveling abroad, check with your physician about any necessary immunizations that may be required. If needed, get them well in advance of your trip in case you have an adverse reaction to any of them.

Gather as much information as possible ahead of time about the places you will be visiting. Whether you travel domestically or internationally, the same personal safety rules apply: Learn as much as you can about your destination and where in those places you should go for assistance—police station, U.S. embassy and so forth.

CARRYING MONEY

When you are planning your trip, estimate as accurately as possible how much money, in cash and traveler's checks, you will need to bring. Try to bring as little as possible in cash, relying instead on credit cards and traveler's checks, so you have a measure of protection if they are lost or stolen. Be sure to record the numbers of all traveler's checks before you leave home and put one copy in a safe place. Take another listing with you on your trip, but keep it apart from the checks themselves.

In addition to a fanny pack or secure purse, travelers should equip themselves with a comfortable money belt or pouch in which cash, traveler's checks and credit cards should be kept. Some of these belts and pouches will accommodate a passport, as well. Several types are available, from the kind that hang around the neck, to a shoulder holster, to the more traditional money belt. Personal comfort should dictate which you use. You can select these items from the safety and travel catalogs listed in the appendix.

CLOTHES SENSE

Your travel wardrobe should be appropriate to the climate and the locale, and should also be comfortable. Avoid wearing clothing that indicates you are a tourist.

Keep the sky-high heels at home. Wear shoes that are sturdy and comfortable, as well as appropriate for your destination. Clothing, like body language, should not communicate double messages. If you don't want to be a target of crime, don't stick out like a sore thumb. Blend in as much as possible.

Inappropriate behavior makes you stand out as much as inappropriate clothing. Show respect for local customs and laws. And if you travel by car, remember that hanging clothes in the backseat or having luggage visible in your car identifies you as a tourist and attracts the attention of thieves.

Travel Documents

Carry the name and policy number of your health insurance company as well as the name and telephone number of someone at home to contact in case of an emergency. Keep your important documents and currency on your person rather than in your luggage, which can get lost or stolen. Use a money belt to hold large sums of cash, your passport and plane tickets safely.

Thieves know that unused tickets are reclaimable for cash. Be wary if a stranger asks to see your ticket, even while you are waiting in line to board the plane. Ticket thieves use the trick of taking a passenger's valid ticket and switching it with a useless boarding pass which they picked up out of the trash container.

Take only those credit cards which are essential to your trip. Make two lists of your credit card numbers and the telephone numbers to call in case they are lost or stolen. One list stays with you (not in your luggage), and the backup list is attached to your itinerary left behind.

Traveling with Children

If you plan to travel with children, begin by gathering the family together to discuss the entire vacation from beginning to end. This makes the children feel part of the process and helps them develop a responsible attitude as well.

Cover the basic principles of safety and security with your children, and teach them what to do if problems arise.

Role-play various situations you think the children may encounter and encourage them to ask questions. To simply say, "Don't talk to strangers," or "Always stay by my side," is not enough. Discussing the *specifics* of what might happen on a trip educates your family and prevents involvement in dangerous situations. Once your children (and you, too) begin to think this way, their level of awareness of potential dangers will be increased.

Every member of your family, including the baby, should carry some form of identification. We take the time to tag our luggage, why not do the same for something far more precious?

The card should include the child's name and where you will be staying as well as any pertinent medical information (blood type, allergies, medications, etc.). Your child can carry her own laminated or plastic-encased card attached to a necklace (worn inside the clothing), or pinned to the inside of a piece of clothing.

If your children become separated from you, using the training you have given them at home, they will know enough to approach and show their identification cards to a police officer, security guard or store clerk for assistance.

Never leave children alone to watch the luggage or save your place in line.

Children should always be accompanied to public restrooms. Also, take them with you when *you* go to the restroom, rather than asking a stranger to keep an eye on them while you're gone.

Never leave young children alone in your room, the lobby, or by the pool. Keep them in sight at all times.

Carry an up-to-date, full face photograph of each child, with pertinent information written on the back: height, weight, age and any identifying marks or characteristics, in case you need to show what they look like to police.

If you are a single parent traveling alone with your children outside the U.S., carry a notarized letter from your former spouse giving his permission to take them out of the country. Without this letter, you could be denied entry into a country if they suspect you of kidnapping.

Teach your children the following:

- The name of the hotel/motel they're staying in.
- Never to go anywhere with a stranger.
- Never to wander off alone.
- To inform you of where they are going and when they will return (if they are old enough to go off alone).
- What to do if lost.

SENIOR TRAVEL SMARTS

The tips in this chapter pertain to all travelers, but here are some additional suggestions especially for the senior citizen:

- Shop around for a reputable travel agency. Some agencies specialize in working with senior citizens. They will even deliver your tickets to your door and provide a shuttle service to the airport.

- When planning your trip, try to minimize the number of connections youll need to make. The more direct the route, the more secure you will be.
- Watch the news for any problems at your destination. Avoid areas of known high crime and political unrest.
- Prepare a detailed itinerary to leave with family or friends so they can contact you if they are concerned about you.
- If your travel plans change for any reason once on your trip, notify your family immediately.
- Carry your insurance card and the phone number of your agent.
- Check to see if your health insurance company covers you wherever you travel. Check your policy for specific language excluding expenses incurred while out of the country. Medicare does not assume responsibility for medical bills once you leave the United States or its possessions. Therefore, look into additional travel medical insurance be*fore* leaving the country.
- Before traveling, carefully assess your health. If you are on a special diet or need special medical care, you may need to bring supplies with you.
- Whether you plan to climb the Mayan ruins, or casually stroll through the outdoor marketplaces of Greece, ask yourself whether you are in physical condition to handle the exertion. If this is more exercise than you get all year, get into shape before you go.
- If you have a serious health condition, travel with a companion who is familiar with your problem.
- Carry a medical summary card specifying your condition, medications and dosages, blood type, names and phone numbers of your doctors, allergies to any medication or insects and any other pertinent information.
- If any of your prescribed medications contain narcotics, obtain a letter from your doctor attesting to your need for them.

- Pace yourself on your trip; plan your activities with rest periods in between.

To obtain more pertinent information and helpful hints, send for the booklet "Travel Tips for Senior Citizens" from:

The Bureau of Consular Affairs
The State Department, Room 5807
Washington, DC 20520

For additional health information, ask for Publication No. CDC 84-8280, "Health Information for International Travel," from:

U. S. Government Printing Office
North Capital Street
Washington, DC 20402

Senior Citizen Travel Groups

September Days Club
P. O. Box 3094
Harlan, IA 51593
(800) 241-5050

Elderhostel
75 Federal Street
Boston, MA 02116
(617) 426-7788

Grand Circle Travel
347 Congress Street
Boston, MA 02210
(800) 221-2610

Chapter 16

❖❖❖❖❖❖

Getting There

Did you know that airports are sometimes the most crime-ridden areas in a city? Not all people at airports are waiting to board a plane; some are there to take advantage of the passengers.

Pickpockets, luggage thieves and other criminals walk among the crowds waiting for an opportunity to make a score. Thanks to unwary travelers, the waiting period is usually relatively short.

Whether you're traveling on business or pleasure, don't be careless and let yourself become a victim of airport criminals.

AIRPORT PARKING

Airport parking lots are targets for car thieves. They're even more vulnerable than mall parking lots since they're open twenty four hours a day, and usually have little in the way of security.

If there is any way for you to get to the airport other than driving there yourself, do it. Theft at airport parking lots is on the increase. Leaving your car in an airport parking lot, even for a short time, can lead to trouble—from losing parts of your car or a tire or two, to having your car stolen.

Take a taxi, bus or train, or get someone who doesn't mind getting up at 4:00 a.m. to take you there. But, unless you have no other choice, don't take your car.

If none of these suggestions is feasible, and you absolutely, positively, have to drive, here are a few tips for safer airport parking.

- Leave the shiny, new car home and take the clunker.

You only have one car and it's a new one? Then try to park it as close as possible to the cashier's booth or the terminal bus pickup area, or in the best lit space in the lot.

- Make sure your car windows are rolled all the way up and the doors are locked. If you have an alarm or an anti-theft device, now's the time to use it.

- Take your parking voucher with you. Don't hide it in the car so you'll be sure to have it when you return. All a person needs to drive your car out of the parking lot is the ticket. A professional car thief certainly won't mind paying a $25.00 or so parking fee to drive off in a late model sedan or sports car, especially when he can dismantle it and sell the parts for a small fortune.

- Don't leave anything of value in your car, and don't think you are fooling anyone by hiding valuables under a blanket. Take out the CD, tape deck, telephone and stereo and leave them at home. Most of these aren't permanent fixtures and can be easily disconnected or released from the dashboard with a few turns of a screwdriver.

- Try disabling your car in the airport lot. There are several ways to do this. If you are not mechanically inclined, ask someone who *is* to show you, for example, how to disconnect the battery.

- If you have a traveling companion, drop that person off with all the luggage before you park you car. If you are traveling alone, stop at the curb and check the bags with a skycap. You want to be able to travel as unencumbered and as quickly as possible from the parking area to the check-in counter.

- Make a note of where you park. You won't want to go wandering alone through acres of parked cars when you return, especially if you have a late night arrival. If you are concerned about walking to your car at night when there might not be many people in the area, ask a cab driver to take you to your car. Give the driver an extra tip to see you safely right to it. It's worth the expense when you consider the alternative.

BAGGAGE BASICS

Hundreds of thousands of bags pass through our country's airports each day, presenting a huge opportunity for theft. Thieves usually look for a baggage carousel where security is lax or nonexistent. Then they hang back with the arriving passengers until the baggage is unloaded. If a bag goes around a few times without being claimed, they take it off and place it on the floor next to them. They wait a few more minutes and if no one shows up to claim it, they pick it up and leave. To reduce the risk of baggage loss or theft, follow these simple safety tips:

Leave the expensive suitcases at home. Nothing puts a smile on a baggage thief's face faster than designer luggage. If the outside is expensive, they figure that what's inside will be valuable. So drag out that scruffy, battered bag you've had for years, lock it, and send it on its way.

Take responsibility for your luggage. If you have a long delay at the airport, use coin-operated lockers. Remember, *you* are responsible for your baggage. Don't be lulled into a false sense of security by having a friendly-looking stranger watch your bags for you while you make a quick trip to the ladies room.

Personalize your luggage. Make every piece of luggage recognizable at a distance. Because luggage tends to look more and more alike these days, even honest people can unwittingly pick up the wrong suitcase.

Mark everything you carry in some distinctive manner. Tie some neon-bright ribbons or woolen pom-poms onto your handles or glue decals to the body of your luggage so you can recognize your bags easily from a distance.

Lock all bags. Lock your suitcases with good, strong locks. If your luggage doesn't come with locks, you can buy inexpensive key or combination locks. The combination type eliminates the possibility that you'll get locked out of your own suitcase if you lose the key. Remember to write down the combination and keep it in a safe place.

Label your suitcases. Airlines require an identification tag with your name and address attached to each piece of luggage you check through, but nobody says you need to put your *home* address and phone number on them. Instead, label your suitcases, inside and out, with a business address (if you have one), or destination address and phone number. Avoid using your home address; it can tip someone off that you are away, leaving your house or apartment open to burglary.

Get rid of old baggage tags. Baggage tags left on from previous trips can lead to misrouting. Check that the three-letter code on your baggage claim check properly identifies your destination airport. Dallas and Dulles sound alike, but there are over 1,000 miles between them.

Check in on time. Check your luggage at least thirty minutes prior to departure (two hours for an international flight). Some airlines will disclaim responsibility for delivering misplaced baggage to your hotel if you check in less than fifteen minutes before flight time.

But checking in too early can also cause problems. If you check your bags too long before departure time, your baggage may be left unattended in the holding area.

Claim your luggage as soon as it is unloaded. As mentioned earlier, thieves hang around baggage carousels waiting to swoop up luggage that nobody appears to be claiming. Don't create this opportunity for them.

Lost or stolen baggage. Fill out a certificate of loss immediately. Don't postpone doing this while you wait to see if your luggage turns up on the next flight. Most airlines require notification within several hours of loss. If you don't turn in a claim before leaving the airport, it will be difficult to blame the airline for any loss or damage. Be sure to get a copy of the report to prove you have filed a claim.

The more baggage you take, the more likely you are to have a problem. Over one million bags are lost every year. The less luggage you carry, the less likely that it will be lost, stolen or damaged.

SCOUNDRELS AT WORK

Be suspicious of strangers at airports. What follows is a not uncommon example of what can happen if you're not.

> "I thought to myself that so far, everything was going according to plan," Gina said.
>
> "I'd made it through all that traffic, found a parking space not too far from the airline terminal, and had only two bags to carry, one of which would be checked through to Chicago. However, because of a long line at the check-in counter, I found myself having to rush to the gate.
>
> "There I was running through the airport, my garment bag slung over my shoulder. All I could think about was David, my fiancé, who

was waiting for me at O'Hare. The last thing I needed was to be stopped in my tracks by a young couple who wanted to know where they could rent a car.

"They looked rushed and frazzled too, so I stopped to explain where to go. They couldn't speak English well, so I had to keep repeating and pointing in the direction of the rental desk. They finally nodded their heads in unison and walked away. I boarded the plane with only a few minutes to spare.

"It was later on the plane, when I tried to pay for a drink, that I realized that my wallet, with all my money and credit cards, had been stolen."

Follow these suggestions to sidestep trouble at the airport:

- Avoid an overly tight schedule. It causes stress and anxiety and sets you up to be a victim. It gives pick-pockets the excuse they're looking for to bump into you and make it look like it's all your fault.

- Keep your eyes glued to your handbag and carry-ons as they come out of the X-ray machine. That's a likely place for a thief to grab your belongings if you are not paying close attention.

- Watch for distractions, such as a staged fight or scattered money. Thieves, working in groups, use these tactics to divert your attention from your purse or baggage long enough for them to abscond with it.

- To keep at least one hand free when you're carrying a lot of luggage, invest in a luggage cart which, when empty, folds down to the size of a small briefcase. Load on your bags, secure the elastic cord, and you're on your way—no fuss, no hassle, no strained shoulder muscles.

AN OUNCE OF PREVENTION (AND ONLY AN OUNCE)

Whether your departure time has been delayed or you've made really good time and have a long wait at the airport before embarking on your trip, there's no reason why you can't wait for your plane in the cocktail lounge. But let common sense be your guide.

A single woman, sitting at the bar, looking around nervously, perhaps having a couple of drinks to ward off anxiety about flying, may be inviting trouble.

Sit at a table, not at the bar. Look relaxed and in charge. Read, doodle in a notebook or seem otherwise busy, but look unapproachable. And, as anywhere else, never flash a wad of bills when it comes time to pay your bill.

If you do have an alcoholic drink, have no more than one. Remember, it's important that you be in control, not the alcohol.

THE INQUISITIVE STRANGER

The plane finally leaves the ground, you settle back into your seat and open the novel you've been dying to read. You've barely read past the first paragraph when your seat-mate starts asking you a lot of personal questions. How should you handle these questions?

Many people use personal questions as a conversation starter. This may seem innocuous enough at first, but how do you stop someone (who is, after all, a complete stranger) from probing into your life history.

When you are in a situation where you cannot easily walk away from someone who is annoying you (as on a plane, bus or train), there are a few strategies you can employ. The art of question-dodging is like the game of tennis. When the ball is in your court, you must see that you get it safely over the net, that it stays in bounds, and that it doesn't come back at you.

> Rosemary, the president and CEO of a midwest consulting firm, unfolded a spreadsheet and placed it on the tray in front of her. She studied the quarterly report and made notes on a separate piece of paper.
>
> "Hey, that looks like quite a detailed report you're working on. My name is Andy Dawes," the young man said, extending his hand. "What's yours?"
>
> "Hello, Andy, my name is Rosemary and no, it's not at all as complicated as it looks."
>
> "Rosemary. That's a pretty name for a pretty lady. Tell me, Rosemary, are you married, engaged, seeing someone...?"
>
> "Look, Andy, I really have a lot of work to do before we land in New York and..."
>
> "Hey, take it easy. I'm only being friendly. No need to get upset with me, okay? How can I get to know you better if I don't ask any questions? So, what do you do for this company?" he asked pointing

to the papers on the tray. "Are you going to New York to meet up with your boss, or what?" he asked, chuckling.

Rosemary looked at him over the top of her glasses, then returned to the papers spread out in front of her.

Andy tried another tactic. "I'm staying at the Hilton. Where are you staying?" Undaunted by her lack of response, he continued on. "We could share a cab if we're staying in the same place or close by and maybe grab a bite to eat one night, if you're available," he added.

"I'll be meeting with clients and conducting business while I'm in New York," Rosemary replied, "and I don't foresee having any free time for socializing." Picking up her pen, she looked directly into his eyes and said, "If you don't allow me to work in peace, I'll ask the flight attendant to change your seat."

You might be wondering what the big deal is about telling a stranger your full name, a few personal tidbits about your life, and where you'll be staying once you land. Think about it this way.

Trade places with Rosemary for a minute. Andy's a nice looking guy, well-dressed and personable. You give him your full name and the name of your hotel. After all, you are single and who knows, this guy may be Mr. Right. What have you got to lose?

Ask yourself whether you can pick a criminal out of a crowd. Do you really think all bad guys go around in torn jeans and leather jackets and have greasy hair. Bad guys come in all sizes and shapes and often can be found clean-shaven, confident and wearing a three-piece suit.

Not *all* the men you meet who are inquisitive about your life are out to harm you. But since you can't tell the good guys from the bad (unlike the way it was in the old-time cowboy movies), you can't afford to take chances. You have to protect yourself from potentially dangerous encounters.

Let's see what might have happened if Rosemary had answered all of Andy's questions.

"Hi, Andy, my name is Rosemary Moore and no, I'm not married or engaged. As a matter of fact, I just broke up with someone I've been living with for three years. Now that I'm back on my own, I've been keeping my nose to the grindstone in Colorado Springs, and I needed to get away for awhile. So even though this is a business trip, I don't see why we can't get together some night. Let me write down the name of my hotel on the back of my business card."

If it turned out that Andy was looking to make trouble, think of the information he would have had to work with: Rosemary Moore is a woman who lives alone in Colorado Springs, who's the president and CEO of the XYZ Company (learned from the business card). She might have money to invest in fraudulent deals. She also might own antiques, silver or fine paintings and jewelry which, if sold on the street, could bring a tidy sum of money. She is staying at a hotel where she can be easily reached and harassed.

To avoid hassles in the future, follow these tips:

- Don't volunteer personal information to strangers. Networking and socializing on planes might seem like a great way to pass the time, but you could be setting yourself up for trouble.

- Decide ahead of time what personal information you should give out to strangers and how you will respond to those questions you don't want to answer.

- If you think you might be interested in getting to know the person who's questioning you, follow the rules in Chapter 4 for meeting a stranger on "safe ground."

- If someone persists in bothering you during a flight, ask the flight attendant for assistance.

TAXI TALES

Taxi drivers are a special breed of human being. Possessing nerves of steel, many of them specialize in the most offensive kinds of driving.

They dart and weave through traffic and drive at breakneck speeds down highways. For them, time is money, and the faster they get you from one place to another, the more money they can make.

To make matters worse, some also play a game that may be dangerous to your wallet. These con artists specialize in transporting out-of-towners. To some cabbies, tourist is just another name for "Easy Mark."

Here are some tips to get you to your destination safely and to deal with dishonest taxi drivers.

- Make sure you have flagged down a legitimate taxi service and not a "gypsy" cab. Licensed cabs are required to display the driver's identification. Be sure the picture is actually that of the driver.

- If you feel that a cab driver is endangering your life by driving unsafely, ask him to slow down or to be less aggressive. If he won't comply, tell him you'll report him to the taxi commission or police department.
- Avoid taking a group taxi with people you do not know.
- If you are traveling alone, never sit in the front of the cab, next to the driver.
- Try to have an idea of your route and an estimate of the correct fare ahead of time. You can ask the hotel for that information when you make your reservation. Or you might ask the reservation clerk at any car rental desk at the airport for the best route to your hotel and the approximate time it should take to get there. At your hotel you can ask the concierge or desk clerk for the same information about any other destinations you may have. Give the driver the impression that you know your way around.
- If you believe you are being taken for a ride, let the driver know it immediately. At the same time, copy down his name and taxi number from the identification card, which should be prominently displayed in the cab.
- When you reach your destination, let him know that although he jacked up the fee by taking you on the scenic route, you will only pay what the fare should have been.

"I took the shuttle from Boston to New York," Nancy began.

"I thought I had everything finally under control, so when I got into the taxi, I took my shoes off and relaxed a bit in the back seat. I must have been daydreaming because when I thought about it, I realized we had been driving for almost forty minutes. Having gone this route several times before, I knew the ride should take no more than twenty minutes.

"I knocked on the glass divider and told the driver to save his joy rides for someone else. He said to me, 'Listen, lady, it looked like you were asleep back there. I thought you'd appreciate the fact I didn't disturb you.'

"When he finally came to my stop, he tried to charge me for all the extra miles. I told him to forget it and tossed the amount I knew it should have cost on the front seat.

"I told him there was no way I was going to let him take advantage of me like that."

What if Nancy's taxi driver had threatened her or refused to give her her luggage unless she paid the amount he asked for? This is what you should do if you find yourself in that situation:

1. Note the time, location, taxi number, license number, name of the cab company and a description of the driver.

2. Pay the full fare and ask for a receipt.

3. File a complaint with the police department, which licenses taxi companies in most cities. (If there is a separate regulating body, the police will tell you what that is.) If you are persistent, you may even be able to get the taxi company to refund the excess fare you paid. At the least, you'll help prevent others from becoming unwitting victims.

Chapter 17

❖❖❖❖❖❖

A Safe Stay

A little effort and thought can make the difference between a safe and pleasant hotel stay and one that makes you wish you'd never left home.

Technological advances in security systems are making hotels safer, from certain standpoints. Computerized locks are replacing the standard room key; the combination is changed after each checkout. And video cameras are sometimes used to monitor garages, elevators, lobbies, entrances and hallways.

But you need to do your part to make your stay safer and more enjoyable.

CHECKING IN

When you arrive at your hotel, do the following to protect yourself and your belongings:

- Stay with your luggage until it is brought into the lobby. If you have a traveling companion, one of you can stay with the luggage while the other goes in to register.
- If you are driving and must park in a garage or parking lot, leave only the ignition key with the attendant.
- While waiting to check in, avoid unnecessary conversations with strangers and don't give out personal information that others may hear.
- When registering, use your last name and first initial only. It's not necessary for your registration to indicate your gender, marital or professional status.

- If a clerk makes an imprint of your credit card when you check in, but you choose to pay in cash when you check out, make sure the imprint is destroyed at that time. An employee could put the bill on your credit card and pocket the cash.

- Don't mention your room number when you are given your key. If the desk clerk loudly announces your room number to the bellhop, quietly explain that you would like a different room (and ask that its number not be announced publicly). If another room is not available, be sure nobody was eavesdropping on you.

- Instruct the desk not to give out your room number. Ask that you be called if someone requests this information.

- If you believe someone is following you when you leave the registration desk, go back to the desk or go to the house phone and pretend to make a call. Speaking of house phones, anytime you use one, turn your back to it and face any possible eavesdroppers while you are talking. This will enable you to see if anyone is listening in on your conversation and should cause that person to walk away. (Actually, it's wise to follow this practice anytime you use a pay phone.)

- Some hotels, for security reasons, give out keys with numbers on them that differ from the actual number of the room. Memorize your room number, or you could find yourself standing alone in a corridor, trying to unlock someone else's door.

- If the porter takes your key and brings your bags to your room by way of a freight elevator, give him a few minutes' head start before you leave the lobby. Let him arrive at your door *before* you do. You don't want to be standing alone outside your room, waiting for him.

- If you are the only one entering the elevator, press the button for your floor *and* several more buttons, so anyone who is watching from the lobby will be unable to tell on which floor you are staying.

- If, for some reason, your key won't open the door, return with the porter *and* your luggage to the front desk to obtain another key.
- If you see someone lingering near your room, report it immediately to the management.

IN YOUR ROOM, AT LAST

You're exhausted after a long trip, and all you want to do is flop down on the bed and relax, but before you do, you'll need to check out a few things and remind yourself of some hints for a safe stay.

- Once inside your room, make sure that the door locks work, that the windows can be secured, that any door to an adjacent room is locked, and that the phone works. Check to see if the switchboard operates 24 hours a day.
- Make it a habit to keep all doors and windows locked, even when you are in the room, and especially when you are in the shower. You can purchase combination travel lock sets that can be used to secure windows, doors, drawers or closets. You may also wish to bring along a special door stop that gives off a shrill alarm if an intruder starts to open your door. And there's a portable alarm that hangs from the inside doorknob and emits a piercing sound if the doorknob is turned from the outside—before the door is opened. A portable deadbolt lock can be inserted in the door without having to use any tools. Check the catalogs listed in the appendix for these items.
- Familiarize yourself with the basic floor plan of your hotel or motel, noting exits, fire alarms and extinguishers closest to your room. In case of a fire, use the stairs, never the elevator.
- Never answer your door without asking who's knocking. If there's a peephole, use it *before* you open the door. If there is no peephole, secure the chain lock, which provides only minimal protection. If someone

knocks at your door and says he's from room service, and you haven't ordered any, call the front desk immediately.

- Each time you leave your room—even for a quick trip to the ice machine—lock your door and take the key with you. It may seem like a big hassle to lock up and carry your key just to go a short distance, but if you don't, consider the possibility that you might be facing an uninvited visitor when you return to your room.

- Whenever you leave your room, day or night, leave a light on. If, on your return, you open the door to an unlit room, close it immediately, go back to the lobby, and ask at the front desk for someone from security to accompany you back to your room. It could be only that the maid turned off the light when she brought extra towels or turned down the bed, but why take the chance that it might be more than that?

- Don't feel secure about leaving valuables in your room just because the door is locked. And don't think you can outsmart thieves by hiding your valuables among your dirty clothes, under the mattress, or in your shoes.

- Consider taking along a fake can of hair spray or foot powder. (They're referred to as "safes".) These are the same as actual product cans, complete with cover and nozzle, but empty. Each has a false bottom which, when unscrewed, reveals a mini-safe. Wrap your jewels in a tissue or piece of cloth, put them into the can, and screw on the bottom. Mixed in with your other toiletries, they're undetectable. You can find these in several catalogs listed in the appendix.

- Or, you can store your valuables in the hotel's safe. Secure the items in a sealed manila envelope and carry it to the front desk as if it contained nothing more than notes from a meeting. Watch your body language so you transmit a relaxed appearance. And remember to get a receipt. It's important to check with the hotel on their liability coverage. Some hotels have only a few hundred dollars' liability limit no matter what the value of items you leave in their safe.

- Put the "Do Not Disturb" sign on your door when you go out for the day. You can help make your room appear occupied by leaving the television or radio turned on.
- When leaving your room, prepare it for maid service, and be sure to secure your belongings.
- Some hotels may request that you leave your room key with them when you go out, to be picked up again upon your return. *Don't do it.* Your schedule is nobody's business.
- Avoid having to fumble for your key by having it in your hand when you return to your room.
- If you are uneasy about entering an elevator or walking the corridor to your room late at night, ask the bellhop or the front desk for an escort. Don't be embarrassed about asking for help.
- Before you turn in for the night, you can make your room a mini-obstacle course for any would-be criminal by moving whatever pieces of furniture you can in front of the door. (Make sure not to booby-trap yourself.)
- Some cities are notorious for thievery, and almost every city has an area that should be avoided. If you plan to walk or jog, check with the desk clerk or concierge about safe areas and times to go. It is also a good idea to bring a fanny pack with some cash and identification, a map and the name and address of your hotel to wear while jogging.
- If your room is broken into, immediately notify the police. Provide them with a complete description of the items stolen (use the inventory list you prepared prior to leaving). Always get a complete copy of the police report to keep for insurance purposes.
- Before you check out, thoroughly search your room for items you may have missed the first time around. Don't forget to retrieve your valuables from the safe at the

front desk. Pay your bill, return your key, and leave those souvenir towels in the room where they belong.

THE MOTEL

If you are staying in a motel, you need to adhere to the same rules as those for hotel safety. But there are some additional cautions to follow, as well:

- Because your car is parked right outside your door, you may be tempted to leave your valuables in the trunk, rather than in your room. *Don't!* Take everything inside with you—even if you are staying for only one night. Don't leave valuables for a thief who will be looking for out-of-state plates or a rental car. Take the time to empty your car. It could save you from having to report a robbery in the morning.
- If possible, park directly in front of your assigned room or in front of the motel office. If you are required to leave your car any great distance from your room, look for another motel.
- Close the blinds before unpacking your luggage—there's no need to display publicly what you brought with you.
- Place all valuables in your trunk *before* you leave the motel, *not* when you arrive at your next destination.

TABLE FOR ONE

Do you look forward at the end of a busy day of sightseeing or business to spending some quiet time alone in your room, just you and your dinner? Or would you prefer to eat out, but concern about dining alone in a restaurant keeps you a prisoner in your room, with only room service to prevent you from starving?

Eating in your room does have its advantages, of course—the main one being that you can dress as comfortably as you wish. Or you may prefer to eat in so you won't have to deal with the possibility of a stranger wanting to keep you company during dinner.

If *that's* what's keeping you in your room, get dressed, gather up a good book to read, a notebook, or some postcards that you've been meaning to write and head out to the restaurant of your choice.

To have an enjoyable dinner for one, keep these few simple tips in mind:

- If you think you might be uncomfortable sitting alone at a table in the middle of the room, ask the host or hostess to seat you at a table next to the wall. You'll feel less conspicuous there.
- To discourage someone from intruding on your meal, read your book or write in your notebook. Look too busy to be disturbed by anyone other than your waiter or waitress.
- If a stranger ignores your "do not disturb" signal and asks to join you for dinner, use a firm tone to quietly explain that you prefer to dine alone. If he persists, ask the manager or server to intervene on your behalf.

Just because you are away from home, don't let all the rules you've established for yourself about meeting new men fly out the window. *You* may be on a holiday, but criminals seldom take a vacation.

If you do decide to allow someone to join you for dinner, at the end of the evening say your good-byes in the hotel lobby. Reject his offer of seeing you safely to your room. Should you decide you'd like to see him again, take charge. You name the time and place and meet him there for coffee or lunch. Proceed slowly and listen to your built-in warning system.

On the other hand, if your time at dinner was more than enough for you, but he asks to see you again, tell him that your schedule doesn't allow for that. Making excuses is defeating and tiring. If the man persists, repeat that your schedule is firm, then walk away. It's simple, really. Why do we have such a difficult time saying "no"—especially to strangers?

TALL, DARK AND DEADLY

Don't assume that because you're away on business, everyone else has business on their minds.

Jean, an obstetrician, was attending an all-day medical conference at a hotel. She related this story.

> "We had broken for lunch and I was standing outside the conference room trying to decide whether I should eat at the hotel or at the little sandwich shop nearby.
> "I noticed one of the panel speakers was heading my way, so I

smiled at him. When he was at my side, I commented on his tan and jokingly asked how he found time to play.

"We stood there talking for a while when he asked me if I would like to have lunch with him. I told him that would be great because I wanted to get his opinion on some of the issues that were being discussed at the conference.

"He said he needed to stop at his suite first to gather some materials for his afternoon presentation and asked me to go with him, saying it would only take a minute. So I did.

"We chatted on the elevator but once inside his suite, his attitude changed. He locked the door, took off his jacket and tie and said, 'Why don't you go to the bathroom and freshen up. I'll be waiting for you in the bedroom.'

"I couldn't believe what I was hearing. When I didn't move, he told me to hurry up, that he didn't have all day.

"When I told him there must have been some mistake, he grabbed my arm and twisted it behind my back and tried to kiss me. We struggled for a bit and I demanded that he let me go. He just laughed.

"He had me pinned against the wall when the telephone rang. He looked at me, then walked over to the phone. I ran out of his room as fast as I could.

"I felt so foolish afterwards for getting myself into a situation like that that I didn't tell anyone what had happened.

"Who would have believed me anyway? He's a prominent and well-respected doctor. I never did return to the afternoon session. I couldn't deal with seeing him again."

Whether you're attending a seminar, conference or workshop, every hotel has a meeting room or conference area in which you can conduct your business. Meet your customers and associates there, not in your room or theirs.

If you have made arrangements to meet a business associate in the lounge area, arrive as close to the appointed time as possible. Should you arrive early for your appointment, sit at a table, not at the bar. Spread your papers on the table and make notes in your notebook to discourage others from approaching you.

If, for some reason, you must meet privately in your room with a man, let someone else in your group know of your plans. And if you are on your own, let the man think that others are aware of this meeting. Don't jeopardize your personal safety, regardless of how "respectable" the person you're meeting with is supposed to be.

Getting Started

Even if you hadn't focused on the subject of personal protection before you started reading this book, by now you undoubtedly realize the need to take charge of protecting yourself and your property.

Take a moment to assess how well you've taken care of yourself in the past. Don't be discouraged if you feel you haven't done enough up until now. That's why you read this book!

Just becoming aware of the problems that exist is a positive step. Your next step is to begin to act on what you have learned.

Look at solutions that will help minimize your chances of becoming a victim. Rethink your old habits. To begin, choose one specific area where you wish to make improvements.

Start today, but *don't try to do everything all at once!*

At home, for example, don't go crazy installing security alarms on every door and window as your first step. Instead, remember to keep your doors and windows locked when you go out. Once this becomes second nature, you can go on to taking other precautions.

In personal protection, what might be difficult to do at first (looking people in the eye when you walk down the street, refusing to give your full name and phone number to a man you've just met) will become easier with practice. Small successes lead to bigger ones.

As you progress in taking control of your safety and well-being, you will add to your accomplishments. The more you take charge of protecting yourself, the less fearful you will be about what might happen to you.

Whether you're at home, on the street, at work or traveling, when you become aware of your surroundings and the people who might threaten you, you can take an active role in keeping yourself from becoming a victim. Confront your fears, recognize your strengths, and claim your right to safety and security.

Knowledge is power. More power to you!

Appendix

Sources for personal protection, home security,
automobile and travel safety items mentioned in this book

Brookstone

5 Vose Road
Peterborough, NH 03458
Catalog; also retail stores in malls
(800) 926-7000

Motion sensor room light, hide-a-key "stone," window bolts, between-studs wall safe, sound and motion-activated light sensors.

Ice, snow and mud tire traction frames, emergency lantern, jumper cables, hide-a-key for the car.

Keyless luggage locks, portable deadbolt, luggage cart.

Magellan's (for Travelers)

Box 5485
Santa Barbara, CA 93150
Catalog
(800) 962-4943

Money and passport belts and pouches, fanny packs, SOS shrill alarm.

Baggage tags, combination and cable locks, luggage carts and straps.

Door stop alarm, "safe" cans, travel lock for hotel doors and drawers.

Travel and safety books.

The Safety Zone

2515 East 43rd St.
Chattanooga, TN 37422
Catalog; retail stores in malls
(800) 999-3030

Personal alarms and whistles, self-defense sprays.

Indoor and outdoor motion sensor lights and alarms, door and window alarms, Charley Bar" sliding window and door lock, door scope (wide-angle peephole), security decals and signs, "fake" alarm system, patio door alarm, front door intercom screener, door jammer, "safe" cans, wall outlet safe, gun lock, home security systems.

Tire inflating air compressor, steering wheel locking devices (The Club and the Kryptonite lock).

Money belts and pouches, hotel doorknob alarm.

Sporty's Preferred Living Catalog

Cleremont County Airport
Batavia, OH 45103
Catalog
(800) 543-8633

Mace.

Vehicle alert, infra-red lighting system, motion detector, door jammer, "Charley Bar" sliding window and door lock, "safe" cans, book safe, wall/floor safe, gun safe.

Ice, snow and mud tire traction frames.

Traveler's Checklist

335 Cornwall Bridge Road
Sharon, CT 06069
Catalog
(203) 364-0144

Money belt and pouch.

Travel lock set, luggage cart, "helping handle" to allow two items (such as briefcase and luggage) to be carried in one hand.

Travel safety book.

Index

A

Acquaintance rape. *See* Rape
Address book, what to do if stolen, 13
Airplanes. *See also* Airports
    handling inquisitive strangers on,
        134-136
Airports
    baggage basics at, 131-132
    crime prevention tips at, 133-134
    parking at, 129-130
    taxi drivers at, 136-138
    waiting at, 133-134.
    watching for strangers at, 132-133
Alarms and security devices
    automobile, 22
    home, 49-51
Alcohol use, and date rape, 36-37
Annual Charity Index, 73
Answering machine, 78-79
    message, while away, 122
Anti-theft devices, for car, 22-23
Assertiveness, in speech, 116. *See also*
        Communication
Automated cash machines, 17
Automobile. *See* Car
Automobile security. *See* Car

B

Babysitter
    instructions to, 85
    your child as, 86
Baggage. *See* Luggage
BankCard Holders of America, 19-20, 74
Basement windows, 49
Body language, 109-110, 115, 117. *See*
    also Communication
Briefcase, tips on carrying, 11

Buddy system, at office, 99
Burglars
    face-to-face confrontation with, 59-60
    protecting home against, 47-54
Burglary. *See* Home security; Security
        systems and alarms
Business associates. *See* Male business
        associates
Business cards, used by criminals, 66
Business meals, and sexual harassment,
        105-106
Business meetings, and sexual harass-
        ment, 145-146
Business phone scams, 99

C

Cabs. *See* Taxi drivers
Car, 27. *See also* Car thieves; Parking
    anti-theft devices for, 22
    approached by someone in, 5
    buying a used, 28-29
    changing locks on, 12
    maintaining dependable, 21-22
    methods of identifying stolen, 22-23,
        28
    protecting yourself against criminal
        in, 25-27
    selling, 29-31
Car thieves, discouraging, 23-24, 27-28
Charity scams, 66, 72-74
Checkbooks, reporting lost or stolen, 12
Checks, paying for purchases with, 17-
        18
Children
    home alone
        answering the doorbell, 83
        coping with outsiders, 82-83
        handling phone calls, 83-84

Guns, cautions against
    carrying, 42
    keeping, in house, 61

H

Handbags. *See also* Purse-snatchers
    choosing safest, 9-10
    protecting, 5, 11, 16, 17
    storing, in office, 96-97
Handguns. *See* Guns, cautions
        against
Handshakes, styles of, 111-112.
        See also Communication
Headphones, walking with, 5, 8
Home security. *See also* Security
        systems and alarms
    checklist for, 52-53
    guns, 61
    hiding your valuables, 53-54
    ploys in gaining entrance, 63-66
    screening people at door,
        66-67, 83
    securing entryways, 47-49
Hospital, going to, for rape exam, 38. *See
        also* Rape
Hotels. *See also* Motels; Vacation
    checking in, 139-141
    dealing with business associates at,
        145-146
    eating alone at, 144
    locking room door, 141
    protecting valuables at,
        142-143
    requesting room at, 123
    screening visitors at, 141-142
    security in, 141-144
House. *See* Home security

I

Identification
    asking for, at door, 66-67
    carrying, 9

for children on vacation, 125-126
Image quotient, testing, 110
Impressions, first, in communicating,
        111
Instincts, trusting, 6
Intercom, wireless, 51-52
Intruder, being confronted by, 59, 60-61
Investments, solicitations of, 71-72

J

Job applications, 89-90

K

Keys
    giving spare to neighbor, 122
    hiding spare, 52

L

Ladies room safety. *See* Restrooms
Latch key children. *See* Children
Locks. *See also* Security systems and
        alarms
    changing, if keys stolen, 12
    door, 48
Luggage
    at airport
        checking, 132
        claiming lost or stolen, 132
        insurance for, 123
        labeling, 131-132
        leaving expensive at home, 131
        locking, 131
        personalizing, 131
        removing old tags from, 132
    in car, 24
    at hotel, 139

M

Mace, 42-43. *See also* Self-defense
Mail order

defense against, 37-38
definition of, 33
facts and fiction involving, 33-34
victim of, 34-35
Rape crisis centers, 39, 43. *See also* Rape
Rape trauma syndrome, 38, 39. *See also* Rape
Relaxation, importance of, in communication, 113-114
Restaurants
business meals with men in, 105-106
eating alone in, 144-145
pickpockets in, 17
Restrooms
safety hints for, 16
watching purse in, 11

S

Safe deposit box, 9, 53
Scams
business phone, 99
charity, 72-74
credit card, 74
investment, 71-72
social security, 18
Security systems and alarms
for car, 22
for home, 49-51
Self-defense
caution about using gun in, 42
handling threatening situations with, 41-42
physical, 43-44
to rape, 37-38
sprays and alarms for, 42-43
training for, 43-44
Senior citizens
travel hints for, 126-128
travel groups, 128
Sexual harassment
boss's responsibilities in, 103
confronting, 106-108
definition of, 101-103

employee rights in, 103-105
guidelines in handling, 107-108
in out-of-town meetings, 106
and meals with business associates, 105-106
and meetings with business associates, 145-146
syndrome, 105
Shopping malls
danger spots in, 15-17
parking at, 15-16
safety hints at, 16-17
Shopping safety
at shopping mall, 15-17
paying, 17-20
Social security card, reporting stolen, 12-13
Social security scams, 18
Solicitations. *See* Scams
Sprays, self-defense, 42-43
Stairways, safety hints for, 16, 53, 123
Steering wheel lock, 22
Stolen vehicle recovery system, 22. *See also* Security systems and alarms
Strangers
handling inquisitive, 5, 134-136
caution about, at airport, 132-133
Street crime. *See also* Muggers; Pickpockets; Purse-snatchers; Rape; Self-Defense
avoiding being a victim, 3-4
choice of handbag, 9-10
handling purse-snatcher, 12-13
kinds of, 6-8
protection of handbag, 11
safety guidelines, 4-6, 8-9
testing potential as victim, 4-6
Suitcases. *See* Luggage

T

Taxi drivers, dealing with, 136-138
Telephone
adult answering, 94-96